HOW TO BE
A GOOD
DIVORCED DAD

HOW TO BE
A GOOD
DIVORCED DAD

Being the Best Parent You Can Be Before, During, and After the Break-Up

Jeffery M. Leving

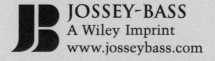

JOSSEY-BASS
A Wiley Imprint
www.josseybass.com

Published by Jossey-Bass
A Wiley Imprint
One Montgomery Street, Suite 1200, San Francisco, CA 94104-4594—www.josseybass.com

Jossey-Bass books and products are available through most bookstores. To contact Jossey-Bass directly call our Customer Care Department within the U.S. at 800-956-7739, outside the U.S. at 317-572-3986, or fax 317-572-4002.

Wiley publishes in a variety of print and electronic formats and by print-on-demand. Some material included with standard print versions of this book may not be included in e-books or in print-on-demand. If this book refers to media such as a CD or DVD that is not included in the version you purchased, you may download this material at http://booksupport.wiley.com. For more information about Wiley products, visit www.wiley.com.

Library of Congress Cataloging-in-Publication Data

Leving, Jeffery.
    How to be a good divorced dad : being the best parent you can be before, during, and after the break-up / Jeffery Leving.—1st ed.
      p. cm.
    Includes bibliographical references and index.
    ISBN 978-1-118-11410-0 (pbk.); ISBN 978-1-118-22420-5 (ebk.);
    ISBN 978-1-118-23750-2 (ebk.); ISBN 978-1-118-24262-9 (ebk.)
      1. Divorced fathers. 2. Parenting. I. Title.
    HQ756.L475   2012
    306.89'2—dc23

                                            2011050954

Printed in the United States of America
FIRST EDITION
PB Printing 10 9 8 7 6 5 4 3 2 1

*For my daughter, who taught me how
to be a good divorced dad and
helped me write this book*

CONTENTS

ACKNOWLEDGMENTS

I couldn't do what I do every single day without the finest team of attorneys assembled under one roof pursuing justice for our clients and their children so they can follow their dreams. Thank you all for your skill and knowledge.

My sincerest gratitude also goes to psychologist Dr. Alan Childs and psychotherapist Dr. Leon Intrater for their insightful and empathetic contributions to this book. They are brilliant at working with divorced dads and their children, and their experience and expertise are invaluable.

Thank you, too, to private detective Wayne Halick for saving and protecting our clients' children without fear for your own safety.

And finally, thanks to Kate Bradford and her team at Jossey-Bass/Wiley for their belief in this book and their advice and support.

HOW TO BE
A GOOD
DIVORCED DAD

INTRODUCTION

When Steven first met with the lawyer he hired to handle his divorce, he told him that he didn't want to try for joint custody of his five-year-old son. When his lawyer asked him why, Steven responded that his wife, Joan, was a good mother and he was the one responsible for the failure of the marriage. "In fact," he said, "I've pretty much failed at everything—I lost my job last year. I'm not a good role model for Joey [his son]. I don't want him to grow up like me."

On further inquiry, the lawyer came to learn that Steven wasn't a failure at all: he had graduated from a top business school and had held a good corporate job until he was downsized along with hundreds of other people in the company. He also sounded as if he was a good father and husband. Steven and Joan's financial problems were the real contributor to the end of the marriage.

"I don't want Joey to see me like I am now," Steven said. "Maybe in a few years, when I get my act together, then I'll try to be more involved in his life."

The lawyer explained the legal facts of life to Steven: that given everything that Steven had told him, joint custody would be possible if he decided to pursue it now, that he should see a therapist to deal with what sounded like depression and low self-esteem, and that once men lose the connection with their children after a sustained period of separation, it becomes more difficult to reconnect on both personal and legal levels.

"You may decide now to forfeit your custody opportunity and in a year or two file a motion for joint custody, but the courts are much more amenable to granting it at the time of a divorce than after years pass. They wonder why you didn't want it from the beginning."

Fortunately, Steven agreed to see a therapist. Even more fortunately, he found a good new job shortly after. He was able to think more clearly about the divorce and decided to seek joint custody, which the court granted. But not everyone is as fortunate as Steven. If you're divorced or in the process of getting a divorce, you may know exactly what I'm talking about.

Many men won't seek out a therapist who can help them with self-esteem issues, depression, and other emotional maladies associated with divorce. Many of these men are out of work or in financial trouble, and it may take months or longer until they get their financial house in order. Many men are so angry about the divorce that they make a series of mistakes—choosing the wrong lawyer, instructing the lawyer they hire to fight a war they can't win, spending money that should be put away for their children's future on expensive and unproductive litigation—that all harm their children.

The odds are that you care deeply about your children and want to do the right thing for them. You want to be the best divorced dad you can be. But the divorce process itself may make it difficult for you to fulfill this objective. You may be too emotionally distraught to make good decisions. You may be a victim of gender bias. You may pursue a legal strategy that isn't in the best interest of your kids.

I'm writing this book to help you avoid the traps and problems that you may encounter in your quest to be a good divorced dad. Let me give you a sense of how my experiences compelled me to write this book.

A Fathers' Rights Crusader

For over twenty-five years, I have fought for the rights of dads in divorce and custody cases. I have built a Chicago law firm that has earned the reputation of one of the premier firms in the country that represents divorcing dads and maintain a Web site, dadsrights.com, to support divorced fathers. I am the coauthor of the new Illinois Virtual Visitation, Right to DNA Testing Notice, Unlawful Visitation or Parenting Time Interference, and Joint Custody Laws, which all improve fathers' rights. In August 2009, I was selected by the White House Office of Faith-Based and Neighborhood Partnerships as an expert resource to join senior White House staff and other community leaders at the first White House Community Roundtable and Town Hall Meeting on Responsible Fatherhood and Healthy Families in Chicago. And I'm a divorced dad.

I note all this not to brag but to impress on you that I get it. I understand what you're going through as a divorced dad, and I have been working most of my adult life to secure you equal rights under the law—and to change the law when equal rights aren't possible.

What concerns me is that it has become more difficult in recent years to be a good divorced dad. This is due in large part to the absent father syndrome. More so than ever before, divorced dads are becoming disconnected from their kids. Here are some statistics that alarm me and I hope also alarm you.

According to just one study from the U.S. Census Bureau, 24 million U.S. children in the United States (34 percent) live apart from their biological father.[1] The United States is now the world's leader in fatherless families. In the early 1970s, Sweden reported the highest percentage of single-parent families. By 1986, the United States had taken over first place in this category, and we have not relinquished this dubious distinction since that time. We now have millions of children growing up without full-time fathers or any father at all in their life. Now consider the following study results:

- Children who live apart from their fathers experience more accidents and a higher rate of chronic asthma and speech defects.

- Seventy-two percent of all teenage murderers grew up without fathers.
- Eight percent of the adolescents in psychiatric hospitals come from fatherless homes.
- Three of four teen suicides occur in single-parent homes.
- The absence of a biological father increases by 900 percent a daughter's vulnerability to rape and sexual abuse. Often these assaults are committed by stepfathers or the boyfriends of custodial mothers.

What's more difficult to measure, but what the other lawyers in my firm and I have observed over and over, is the increase of emotional absence. Many divorced dads are not involved in the decision-making process that affects their kids. They often don't see them as much as they are entitled to, and when they're with them, some are spending much of their time with their children watching television and not communicating. A depressed dad has difficulty being a good dad, and a financially broke, out-of-work dad has trouble feeling good enough about himself to parent effectively. Divorce combined with societal gender bias exacerbates these negative feelings, but it doesn't have to be this way. This book will help you change things for the better.

What's In It for You . . . and Your Kids

In the following pages, you'll find advice that will help you become a good divorced dad and stories that illustrate how others have done so and succeeded.

Some of the advice is legal, such as information about legal strategies to obtain custody, parenting, or visitation rights; the importance of language specificity for dads in divorce agreements; how to find the right lawyer for your situation; and ways in which you can make a case for sole custody if you feel your wife or the new man in her life is a danger to your children.

Some of the advice is personal. Although I'm not a psychologist, I work closely with two psychologists, and they contributed a great deal to this book. In addition, lawyers who have worked extensively with divorcing dads come to be savvy about how a client's psychological makeup affects their legal approach. I know the dangers of both depression and anger when it comes to making smart decisions about custody, visitation, and support. So the advice here is designed to help you get in the right frame of mind to do right by yourself and your children. In some instances, this may mean exercising extreme self-control when you're in the presence of your ex. In other instances, it may mean working with a therapist to address the emotional obstacles preventing you from being fully present in your child's life.

The stories in this book cover both legal and personal territory. They are drawn from my experiences representing clients as well as those of my firm's attorneys and other attorneys outside our firm. I have changed the names and some of the details because of attorney-client privilege, but the basic elements of the stories are what took place. Some of the stories offer cautionary lessons about mistakes divorcing dads make. Others will motivate you to take the steps necessary to become more involved with your kids. I think all of them will resonate with you, since they capture the hopes and frustrations of most fathers who are going through divorce.

Finally, let me impress on you my belief that just about everyone has the ability and the desire to be a good divorced dad. Perhaps a tiny percentage are just bad people and don't care about their kids (and never should have had them in the first place), but the overwhelming majority want nothing more than to be a loving, involved parent. The first step to achieving this goal is becoming aware of and overcoming the obstacles that stand in the way—the subject of the first chapter.

CHAPTER 1

The Obstacles

*Identify the Factors That Can Drive a
Wedge Between You and Your Children*

If you're like most other divorced dads, you want to see your children as much as possible. In an ideal world, you and your ex would split the time you spend with them fifty-fifty, and you'd make sure that every moment you have with them is quality time.

Unfortunately this ideal is difficult to achieve for many reasons. Most obvious, if the custody agreement limits you to the traditional schedule of every other weekend and one night a week, you can't be with your kids as much as you want. Less obvious, if your self-esteem is low, you may be with your kids in body but not in your heart and mind—you're not engaging with them fully. In either instance, the outcome is bad for your children and bad for you. No matter what you've heard or what you've told yourself, kids need their dads.

Even if you think that dads have a crucial role to play, you may have resigned yourself to partial or complete absence. Maybe you believe that the obstacles that keep you from having the relationship you want with your children are too big to overcome.

Or maybe you look at the obstacles and figure it would take too much time, money, and effort to clear the way for you to spend more time with your son or daughter.

In fact, most obstacles can be overcome, and in many instances, you don't have to possess unlimited resources to overcome them. I've helped dads who weren't seeing their children at all or were seeing them infrequently and watched them become fully involved parents relatively quickly. I've observed dads who had poor or no relationships with their kids make changes in their attitudes and actions and become great parents with great relationships.

The first step in this process is identifying and understanding the obstacles that stand in the way of being fully present in your children's lives.

The Seven Obstacles to Being Fully Present in Your Children's Lives

The following list of obstacles is far from inclusive. I've focused on the seven most common ones, but probably four or five times this number exist. One or several of these seven, however, are likely to apply to you. As you'll see, some of these obstacles are legal, some are emotional, and some have to do with the ex-spouse. As you read the discussions of each obstacle, think about which ones may be preventing you from being completely present with your children:

1. The terms of the custody agreement
2. Orders of protection
3. Financial problems
4. Legal trickery
5. Gender bias
6. Guilt
7. Anger

If these obstacles seem formidable—and if they cause you to think of all the more specific reasons you are unable to see your children as often as you want—keep in mind that you're not in this alone or without support. More judges are starting to recognize the importance of dads being a consistent, integrated presence in their children's lives. In fact, it's not unusual for some judges to emphasize this point to both parents—to remind dads to make the effort to be involved and to remind moms that even if they're furious with their ex, their children's welfare comes first.

Second, find a lawyer who is well versed in dads' rights and can help you deal with everything from baseless orders of protection to gender bias. They understand the law, they are savvy, and they know how to help you overcome the nonlegal obstacles that might get between you and your kids.

Third, good therapists who have experience with and expertise in the struggles divorced dads go through can provide significant assistance, not just with making custody and visitation recommendations but to help dads overcome the emotional barriers to parenting.

Let's turn to the first obstacle and examine what it is, how it affects divorced dads, and how you can overcome it.

Obstacle #1: The Terms of the Custody Agreement

Many men are saddled with bad custody agreements, especially ones lacking joint custody or custodial parent status. The typical bad agreement restricts them to infrequent contact with their kids, either because of weak legal advocacy or their having given up hope. As a result, they become de facto absent dads because there's not enough time to bond with their kids. These dads often feel terribly hurt after the dust settles, and the realization of what's happened to them and their relationship with their children sets in. Later I'll address the specific tactics to prevent bad custody agreements from happening, but for now, the most basic piece of advice is to try for joint custody (or sole custody if that's a better option). Dads with joint custody have a good chance to maintain strong relationships with their kids.

It's certainly understandable for divorced dads to feel this way. After having their kids under the same roof for years and seeing them every day, this new arrangement often feels punitive and destructive to the parent-child relationship. But in some cases, fathers can do something about an agreement that's already been set. Certainly if the agreement is unconscionable for some reason, circumstances change radically, or the ex-spouse is endangering the kids, the dad can go back to court.

But let's assume that none of this is true and you're saddled with whatever custody agreement has been handed down by the court. In these instances, you can do three things that will help you overcome the distancing effect of the agreement.

First, *capitalize on your ex-spouse's need for help with the kids on certain days and at certain times*. No matter what the visitation schedule dictated by the agreement is, the reality is that life throws things at us that present opportunities. There are times when your child's mother will be sick, will have to work late, will be traveling, and so on. If you wait for her to ask for your help, she may turn to a friend or relative instead. Volunteer to help out with the kids. When she tells you that her boss has been asking her to do more travel for work, say, "I'll be glad to take the kids when you're gone if that would help out." You have to be proactive: watch for opportunities when she will welcome your assistance with the kids. And absolutely do not preface your offer of assistance by saying something to the effect of, "You know, I really think I should have the chance to spend more time with the kids." This may make your ex-wife defensive or even angry, and she might respond with something like, "Well, if you wanted to spend more time with them, why were you gone so much when we were married?"

If you have a sharp lawyer, the language in your custody agreement may facilitate this type of additional visitation opportunity. Specifically, that agreement could say something to the effect that your court-ordered visitation is the minimum visitation schedule and that your ex-spouse must offer you additional visitation during all time periods your children won't be in your ex-spouse's care.

Second, *overcoming visitation obstacles presented by the agreement requires making the effort to create quality time*. Divorced dads want to spend quality time with their kids, but they often don't do the planning or try to be as involved in activities as they could be. Again, this is understandable, but it's not acceptable. You may well have good reason to feel resentful about the divorce and the custody agreement, but move past it and focus on your kids. It's your responsibility to turn the time you do have into experiences that are meaningful and memorable for them. Think of things you can do together. It doesn't have to be anything fancy; you can visit museums, have dinner a restaurant, go hiking, or whatever activities interest them. You might not get more time with them, but the time will feel much more satisfying to you and the kids. It will be quality time.

Third, *cultivate a good relationship with your ex*. For some of you, this may not be difficult: your relationship ended on reasonably civilized terms—maybe even amicably. Some of you, however, may despise your ex because she was unfaithful, cruel, or vindictive or she behaved badly in other ways. If she's a decent mom, however, try to hide your animosity and be civil when you communicate with her (or about her to others, including your children). Even if she isn't particularly civil to you, be the better person. The odds are that your relationship with your kids will benefit them in the long run, if not in the short term, since your ex will eventually be more willing to bend the terms of the custody agreement in your favor (at least some of the time). Although it may not seem like it now, time heals at least some of the wounds from the marriage, and you want her to be more amenable to your wishes, especially regarding time with the kids. Maintaining a civil relationship with your ex is one way to make this outcome more likely.

Obstacle #2: Orders of Protection

It is becoming increasingly common for moms to have their lawyers obtain orders of protection against dads as part of a legal strategy. Many times, there is little or no basis for these orders, yet unscrupulous lawyers can sometimes get moms to agree to testify that they feel their spouses are a danger to them or the kids. It may be that when mom broke the news to dad that she wanted a divorce (perhaps because she was in love with someone else), he became angry. Maybe he shouted at her or threw something or said, "You'll regret this." All this can be used as the basis for an order of protection, even if the father was not putting anyone in danger.

Similarly, some dads arrive home one day and find the police there telling them they can't enter. Their wife has gone to court without providing notice to them and obtained emergency ex parte (for one party) orders of protection. Dads who ignore the order and enter the home may end up being incarcerated. These orders can often be easily obtained in court with no notice or opportunity for the dad to be in court and defend himself. The judge hears one side of the story and makes a critical decision.

And even more egregious, some women file false charges of abuse, claiming their husbands physically or sexually hurt them or the kids. Again, hurtful as it can be to an innocent father, this is rationalized by some as a legal strategy: everyone is doing it, it doesn't mean anything, it's simply a means to an end, and so on.

These strategies, however, can have devastating consequences not just for the dads they're used against but for their children. They can cause men to feel guilty and despicable even when there's no reason for them to feel this way. It can also make them believe that they are bad dads who don't deserve to spend time with their children.

If you find yourself on the receiving end of a manufactured order of protection or false abuse allegations, consult your lawyer. In civil cases, good divorce lawyers may recommend petitioning the court to order your wife to submit to a psychological evaluation. If she's obviously so angry about the divorce or related issues that she's taking these actions to seek revenge, a therapist may recognize this fact and testify about it in court. If there are criminal charges brought against you, though, you may not be entitled to this degree of legal preparation in a criminal case, and you'll need to file an appropriate civil action in your pursuit of justice.

In worst-case scenarios, some lawyers, together with gender-biased therapists, convince dads to admit in court to abuse they didn't commit. This may sound implausible, but I've seen a number of instances in which this has taken place. Typically it happens when the dad is indigent, uneducated, or disadvantaged in some other way, and the opposing attorney conspires with the therapist or some other individual to communicate the following message: "Look, we know you didn't abuse your child, but given the circumstances, the judge is going to believe you did and never let you see your child again if you don't confess. So if you admit to the abuse and pledge to the judge that you won't let it happen again, the court will feel you're taking responsibility for your actions and eventually let you have visitation with your child."

I recognize it's unlikely that you would fall for this ploy (and if you have a competent attorney, he or she will make sure you don't fall for it), but I relate this story to illustrate how divorced dads can become overly compliant and even masochistic. If your spouse pursues an order of protection against you that is unwarranted, don't just accept it because you feel you should be punished even though you've never threatened your wife or child. The other side may paint you as a villain who shouldn't see your child much or at all, but if their portrait is false, then you need to stand up for your rights and your child's rights. Don't become a target looking for an arrow.

Obstacle #3: Financial Problems

Your bank account balance shouldn't determine your self-worth, and in the same way, your ability to support your family shouldn't define you as a dad. Nonetheless, many dads equate the two measures, and when they find themselves unable to meet support payments or support their kids in the way they could prior to the divorce, they allow it to interfere with their parenting. Their lowered self-esteem makes them uneasy and ashamed in the presence of their children. They don't like that feeling, so they don't see their kids as often as in the past.

Don't fall into this trap.

Perhaps the most insidious circumstance involves financially strapped dads who, voluntarily or by order of a court, end up being cut off completely from their children. Here's how it typically happens. Dads know they don't have the money to make the anticipated child support payments; they may not even have sufficient funds to hire an attorney to handle the divorce. Embarrassed and ashamed, they walk away—they become "dead-broke deadbeat dads" and flee the state and start over somewhere else. A default judgment is entered against the dad, mandating that he pay support he can't pay and that he not be afforded visitation privileges. Eventually he is found in contempt and sentenced to jail. It becomes a self-fulfilling prophecy.

Just as typically, this dad misses his kids. He eventually finds a job and accumulates some money and decides he wants visitation. But when he goes back to court, he is handed a whopping bill because of all the previous payments he missed. He doesn't have enough money and is incarcerated based on the prior order.

Don't let it reach this point. Recognize that even if you're out of work, you can petition the court to take your economic circumstances into consideration and order a lower support payment that is feasible for you. Certainly the court will expect you to search diligently for a job, and once your income increases, so may your support payments. But don't feel as if you shouldn't see your children because you can't buy the toys they want. Your children will miss your presence much more than any toys you would have given them. Your ex-wife may berate you for losing a job, but the bond you have with your children can withstand a diminished paycheck. Sooner or later your financial situation will improve, so don't make decisions like ignoring the legal process and your child support obligations that you'll regret for the rest of your life.

Obstacle #4: Legal Trickery

If you have a highly skilled, shrewd divorce lawyer, this obstacle shouldn't be a problem. Unfortunately, many men lack good divorce lawyers for a variety of reasons. I'll get to those reasons in a moment and tell you the mistakes to avoid, but first let's examine why legal shenanigans from the opposing attorney can turn into an obstacle. Specifically, there are three common ploys to be alert for.

Changing Jurisdiction

Typically what happens here is that the wife asks to take the child to visit relatives in another state before the divorce action is filed as a ploy to change jurisdictions. She says she needs a break, that it would be good for both her and the child to get away and see her parents. When she tells the husband she doesn't know how long she's going to be there but it probably won't be more than a week or two, he figures there's nothing wrong with letting them go. If the dad feels guilty about the marital discord, he's especially vulnerable to this ploy and will probably accede to her request.

This father (and his incompetent attorney) are not aware of the Uniform Child Custody Jurisdiction and Enforcement Act, which presumes jurisdiction for the divorce-linked custody case being in the state where the child has resided for the last six months; therefore, making it a race to the courthouse. If the mother's lawyer files for divorce and custody first after a minimum of six months has passed, then jurisdiction to determine the appropriate state to litigate custody will occur in the new state where that lawyer files. This new state is where the mother took the child to allegedly visit relatives but now claims it as their residence. When this happens, the father is placed at a huge disadvantage that can often lead to losing custody and maybe even contact with his children. For one thing, he may not be able to afford to keep flying back and forth to that state during the drawn-out jurisdictional proceedings. Second, the lawyer the wife hires there will be familiar with the judges and system in that state, and the father's attorney probably won't have that same familiarity. The bottom line is that this dad and his lawyer may have fallen into a complicated legal trap.

Manufacturing Conflict Between Parents

Joint custody is one of the best ways to avoid the absent father syndrome, but manipulative divorce lawyers who represent custodial parents know that if they can demonstrate in court that the parents can't agree on anything regarding their kids, the judge will more likely block requests for joint custody from the noncustodial parent. A well-coached mom can create so much conflict with her spouse about so many issues that the judge will probably determine that joint custody would be a disaster, even if most of these conflicts never existed before and are being manufactured for the judge's benefit. She can pick fights with her spouse in court and suggest that she and her husband can't agree about what the children should eat, bedtimes, Internet policy, and so on. If the judge believes that they will be at each other tooth and nail over every aspect of their kids' lives, he'll likely rule against joint custody in the best interest of the child. Such a ruling can be very unfortunate for the children.

Fleeing the Country

Some moms are so furious with their spouse or so narcissistic as parents that they may opt for exile. Advising a client to leave the United States contrary to a court order and to avoid sharing the child in any way with the other parent advocates parental kidnapping. Nonetheless, conniving divorce lawyers know that people can likely flee the country without repercussions, provided they go to the "right" country. By "right," I mean countries that are not signatories to the Hague Convention, an international treaty designed to prevent these types of international parental kidnappings. For instance, Japan is a nonsignatory country, so it is very difficult to get a child back who has been taken there by a parent. Obviously this is a radical strategy, but it does happen. I know of one inexperienced lawyer who advised his client to allow his wife and child to leave the country for a visit with her relatives there. This lawyer naively assumed that her desire to see relatives was sincere and that she had no ulterior motive. When she failed to return and refused to return all correspondence, this lawyer realized he had made a terrible mistake.

Many other legal machinations exist, and we'll look at a number of them in the following chapters. For now, recognize that your wife's lawyer may be unethical, or your wife, out of malice or for other reasons, may decide to take advantage of legal loopholes and deprive you of your parental rights.

To guard against being thwarted by this obstacle, make sure you have a divorce attorney experienced in these matters. Too many times, men ask their business attorneys to represent them in the divorce. They figure that "an attorney is an attorney," that they trust their business lawyer, they know this person is smart, and they figure their divorce case is cut and dried. Sometimes they are right. Sometimes, though, they are wrong, and they regret it for the rest of their lives.

Obstacle #5: Gender Bias

Therapists, lawyers, and judges can demonstrate gender bias. By this, I mean that they can provide recommendations, strategies, and judgments that reflect their prejudice—usually in favor of women and against men. I'm not suggesting that all or even the majority of these professionals are guilty of gender bias, but I have seen enough of it over the years to know that it's not uncommon and that it can increase the odds of father absence.

If you or your attorney suspect bias, consider an investigation to see if a given professional exhibits a pattern of biased actions. For instance, we know that certain therapists consistently recommend that women be given custody and that men be denied joint custody or be given restrictive visitation privileges. In these instances, we petition the court for another therapist. At the very least, if you have any doubts about the recommended therapist, your lawyer should consider doing a background check to make sure this person's credentials are in order. When we've conducted these investigations, we've discovered that some therapists have obtained their degrees over the Internet from unaccredited universities or that they have something in their background that makes them unsuitable for divorce and custody cases.

Judges, like therapists, can also be gender biased. In one horrific case, a dad was dealing with a suicidal wife who had multiple lovers. Ample evidence existed on both counts, and it seemed that this man would get custody: he was a responsible, loving father and the mom was clearly unfit to be the custodial parent. The judge nevertheless awarded custody to the mom.

When judges are biased like this, lawyers should consider pursuing what is called a motion for substitution of judges (in the previous case, the inexperienced lawyer representing the dad was learning his craft and so didn't realize this was an option). Some experienced lawyers, however, are reluctant to make this motion, fearing it will anger the judge sufficiently that he or she will be biased against them in future cases. Avoid lawyers who are unable or unwilling to represent you zealously and correctly.

Obstacle #6: Guilt

This may seem a less formidable obstacle than the others, but in its own way, it's far more insidious. Most men are raised to feel responsible for their families. They've been socialized to believe that they should be the breadwinners. The media have done many stories about deadbeat dads and excoriated them for failing to live up to their financial responsibilities. Certainly dads should live up to these responsibilities, but in some instances, they lack the money to do so: they've lost jobs, for example, or have incurred significant financial debt or are experiencing costly health problems. When dads lack the financial resources to make their child support payments, a surprisingly large percentage walk away from their kids. They feel so guilty about not being able to meet their financial obligations that they can't face their children.

This is the worst possible response to guilt. It is far more dangerous to walk away than to acknowledge your financial difficulties and remain in your children's lives. Yet this guilt is difficult to overcome, especially if you blame yourself for the failure of your marriage and the negative effect it's having on your kids. To understand the power of guilt to separate dads from their kids, here are two illustrative stories.

Jerry came home early from work and discovered his wife, June, in bed with his neighbor. Although he found out that she had been having an affair for some time, he blamed himself for it. He told me he was convinced that his inattention and problems holding on to a good job had "forced" his wife to cheat on him and that he didn't want to try for joint custody or even see his kids much until he went through therapy and figured out his career.

Mark was even guiltier and in even greater denial than Jerry. Prior to the divorce, Mark's wife emptied their bank accounts, had an affair, and told their kids that their dad was a jerk and that they'd be better off without him. Incredibly, Mark justified her saying terrible things about him to their children by thinking that he had failed his wife, that he was overweight and not attractive to her, that he spent too much time on the road for his job and she was lonely, and that he had yelled at her because of her overspending. In their divorce case, he wanted to agree to her terms, which were blatantly unfair and included a miserly visitation schedule with the kids. Essentially he wanted to punish himself, and he was using the divorce settlement and visitation as a way to do it.

But the most guilt-inducing situation for a divorced dad happens when the mom is a classic parental alienator who has been speaking negatively about him to the kids. Perhaps she has told the kids that their father is the reason they can't go to camp this summer ("he's not giving us enough money") or that he is the one who tore the family apart. The children can't help but be affected by whatever she says. One day one of the children becomes angry about something the father has said or done and says, "I don't want to see you anymore."

Trust me when I tell you that if your child says something like this to you, he doesn't really mean it, at least not in the way you think. He may not want to see you in that moment when he's angry, but it doesn't mean he won't ever want to see you again. Many dads, however, react by thinking, *He's right; I'm doing more harm than good as a parent. I'll respect his request and stay away.*

Obstacle #7: Anger

While some dads are vulnerable to guilty feelings, others are more susceptible to rage. Anger can erect major barriers to strong parent-child relationships, especially when this anger is persistent and deep. It's not unusual for one or both parties in a divorce to be angry. Sometimes people become angry as they argue over who gets what—a dispute over a favorite painting or piece of furniture can trigger major arguments. It's also typical for the person who asked for the divorce to earn the enmity of the other spouse, and this anger is especially acute if the reason for the divorce was that one person was having an affair.

This anger, though, doesn't always affect children after the divorce is finalized and both people go their separate ways. Angry dads often calm down once their lives stabilize, they meet someone else, and they find that they still can see and enjoy their kids on a regular basis.

In some instances, though, anger at a spouse persists and even builds. This happens for many reasons, from jealously of a spouse's financial circumstances (perhaps she has a rich boyfriend) to bitterness over what she is telling the kids about you. It may also spiral out of control based on what your children tell you about your spouse. For instance, they may describe how happy she is since she met a wealthy guy who buys her presents all the time and takes the family on great trips. And what really gets a dad's blood boiling is when they refer to the new boyfriend as "Dad."

Some men transfer the anger they feel toward their wives to their kids. They feel their children are taking their ex-wife's side and are furious at their lack of objectivity and don't see them out of spite. They may also have gotten into vicious verbal arguments in front of their children, and so to protect their kids from these angry fights, they stay away.

If you allow your anger to drive a wedge between you and your children, you'll regret it. Sooner or later, that anger will ebb, but you may have done irreparable damage to the relationships you have with your son or daughter in the interim. You should realize that your rage is something therapists are often good at dealing with, especially if they are specialists in anger management. Seek counseling if you find that your anger is preventing you from seeing your kids or engaging with them regularly and meaningfully. Recognize that you may have a right to be angry at your spouse, but you shouldn't let it interfere with your relationship with your children.

Question Your Rationalizations

Rationalizations help keep the seven obstacles in place. Consciously or not, divorced dads often create arguments for themselves about why it's better for their children if they stay away rather than visit more frequently. They convince themselves that they don't deserve time with their sons and daughters or that their kids don't really need or want to spend time with them. Although there are some facts of divorced life that you may not be able to change—you live apart from your children, you see them on only certain days and at certain times—you can take actions that enable you to overcome many of the obstacles that divorce and your own feelings place in your path.

Questioning your rationalizations helps you take these actions. Once you become aware that you're not doing what is in your children's best interest by staying away, you gain the perspective necessary to act differently and in ways that benefit not only your kids but yourself. Look at the following questions and see if any of their rationalizations apply to you:

- Do you fail to provide your attorney with information that might help you gain better visitation terms because you don't think anything you do will help restore your formerly healthy relationship with your kids?

- Do you passively accept whatever your ex-wife tells you visitation will be because you don't feel you have a right to state your case?

- Do you hire an attorney who has little experience in family law because you don't think anything an attorney will do can make a difference?

- Do you spend most of the time you have with your kids watching television because you figure they don't really want to talk with you about anything significant?

- Do you believe that your attitudes and behaviors resulted in the divorce and "breaking up the family," and do you feel you should suffer because of it?

- Do you get frightened by how angry your ex-wife makes you, and do you sometimes avoid both her and the kids so the children won't witness your verbal battles?

- Do you encounter gender bias from a judge or therapist and figure it's justified because kids need their mothers a lot more than they need their fathers?

- Do you fail to show up at key events in your kids' lives because you are convinced they view you as an embarrassment and prefer you don't attend?

- Do you tell yourself that your kids need a break from you and that your absence for sustained periods of time will allow the emotional wounds of the divorce to heal?

If any or all of these rationalizations apply to you, you need to take whatever steps are necessary to get past them. For some people, pasting the questions up where they're highly visible helps as a reminder that they're rationalizing in ways that are detrimental to their role as a parent. For others, talking about them with a friend, family member, or therapist is useful. These objective third parties they trust can make them aware of the fallacies in their thinking.

Of all the rationalizations, though, the last one can do serious damage to a relationship with your kids. The longer you cut yourself off from your children, the more difficult it is to reestablish contact. As we'll see in the next chapter, make every possible effort to connect with your kids. They need you.

CHAPTER 2

The Difference Between Good Dads and Struggling Fathers

Being a good divorced dad requires conscious effort. An adversarial divorce process often conspires to turn fathers with good intentions into ones who behave harmfully toward both their ex-wives and their children. When men are separated from daily contact with their children, become victims of gender bias, suffer from low self-esteem because of punitive court rulings, or are manipulated by their ex-wives, they often react badly.

For instance, moms may inform dads that their children blame them for the divorce, deliberately distorting the truth in order to inflict emotional pain on their ex. Dads are vulnerable to these accusations and may feel guilty, even though both partners were equally responsible for the divorce and the children don't blame one parent more than the other. They may believe they failed their children even when they have not and decide that their kids would be better off spending much more time with the mother than with them. For this reason, they agree to a custody arrangement and visitation schedule that provides them with less time with their children than they might normally obtain under the law. These dads want to do the right thing for their kids, but the mom's manipulated court order prevents them from exercising the visitation with their children that the kids require for their emotional stability and their health.

In reality, children need their dads to get past their low self-esteem, vengeful feelings, and other negative emotions. That's often the only way they can be fully present in their kids' lives and protect them.

Most fathers are well aware of what their children need from them and meet this need. Unfortunately, divorce can cloud this awareness. For some divorced dads, what seems like the right thing to do is actually the wrong thing. For others, it's difficult to know what is the right thing. Under tremendous stress, both financial and emotional, many men lose perspective on their critical role as dads. They may be good dads in certain respects, but in other areas, they fall short.

This chapter sets out what constitutes good dad versus struggling dad behavior. Obviously situations vary, and what might be the right thing for one dad to do is the wrong thing for another, so what I can do is define success and failure for most dads in most situations. In this way, you're more likely to know the right thing to do in the situations most men encounter during and after the divorce.

Choice of Attorneys

This isn't about getting the toughest lawyer that you've heard will really stick it to your spouse. In fact, good divorced dads often do the opposite: they focus on finding family law experts who genuinely care about what's best for the children and the client.

Don't let your anger dictate whom you hire for an attorney. Recognize that you're vulnerable to lawyers who may play on this anger when they say that they're going to make your wife sweat and that they'll put her through a trial that will make her "regret ever filing for divorce." As satisfying as that may seem in the short term, it's not what you or your children need in the many years that will follow.

Let me give you an example of what happens when a dad hires an attorney who is well known for being overly aggressive and for creating conflict. John, furious at his wife, Joan, because she was having an affair with a colleague, chose an attorney because he had a cutthroat reputation for a no-holds-barred approach. Joan, a high-powered corporate sales executive, was in a meeting with a customer when a big, burly policeman who moonlighted as a process server barged into the meeting and served her with the court papers. Joan was humiliated, and this humiliation translated into her hiring an equally combative attorney. The animosity generated at the trial remained long after the divorce case ended, and it resulted in numerous verbal altercations in front of their children.

Good dads make hiring a child-focused attorney a priority and monitor whether that attorney considers the best interest of the child throughout the divorce process. One simple and effective way to do this is to pose scenarios to a prospective attorney during your interview process. We do this all the time when trying to find the right attorneys for our firm, and you can use the same method.

Ask an attorney if he would ever instruct a process server to embarrass your spouse by serving her at her place of employment or in the presence of your children; or if he would use a trial to subject her to the kind of humiliation on the stand that you suffered in your marriage; or if he would take her deposition to ask her irrelevant questions only to make her uncomfortable and angry.

Good dads avoid attorneys who seem to relish vendettas. If, during the interview, an attorney tells you stories about how he made one client's wife squirm and how he tore apart another one during the divorce trial for pure enjoyment, this is probably not the attorney for you. Don't get me wrong. In some instances, you need a strong, aggressive attorney on your side. Some divorce cases turn into wars, and in these instances, you need someone to protect your interests—not to mention the interests of your kids. But you don't want to turn a potentially simple divorce into a war.

There is a saying: "A bad settlement is often better than a good trial." Settlements can be better for financial reasons, but beyond that, they often are able to limit the animosity between spouses that trials exacerbate. You need to make every effort to maintain a civil relationship with your ex-spouse, no matter whether you believe she deserves your civility.

Mediation

In many areas of the country, mediation is mandatory in custody cases. Mediation is nonadversarial (at least in theory), whereas custody litigation is highly adversarial; the former attempts to help both parties find common ground outside the courtroom, while the latter may involve a winner-loser courtroom paradigm. Again, the legal process may not make you favorably disposed toward mediation. Cynicism can cause fathers to see mediation as part of a system rigged to delay or deny them access to their children. Anger can cause them to see it as part of a process designed to humiliate them further. As a result, they go through mediation raging against their spouse or being uncooperative in other ways; some dads blow it off altogether, never attending any of the sessions. These actions not only ratchet up tension with their spouse but may result in a judge's denying or limiting the time they're allowed to spend with their sons and daughters, even when they are badly needed by their children.

Good dads make good-faith efforts to participate in mediation for two reasons. First, they recognize that if custody-related issues are resolved amicably in mediation rather than through litigation, the kids are spared a lot of stressful situations, from courtroom drama to out-of-court histrionics. Second, they understand that their "performance" in mediation may get back to the judge and can have a positive impact on his decision.

I had a client, José, who had anger management issues as well as attention deficit disorder, both of which were exacerbated by the divorce process. Though José was a good person who loved his children very much and wanted to be with them as much as possible, he didn't come off as this type of person during the mediation sessions, partly because he refused to prepare for mediation with a mental health professional as counselor. At times, he appeared distracted and disinterested. At other times, he took his anger out on the mediator. The mediator reported to the judge that José seemed to be verbally abusive and could possibly be a danger to his children. As a result, he not only didn't receive joint custody but his limited visitation was supervised.

José ignored our advice prior to mediation, but if you want to increase the likelihood of being an involved father, you'll heed these do's and don'ts:

Do

- Get help prior to mediation from a mental health professional to control your anger if that's a challenge.
- Make an effort to be an involved, calm participant, even if you believe that your wife's attitude and actions will make mediation useless.
- Communicate that you intend to put your child's interest before your own; state specific things you will do that prove this point.

Don't

- Try to convince the mediator that your wife is in the wrong and you're in the right.
- Obsess about what you are entitled to and fail to mention what your kids deserve.
- Show up late to mediation sessions, fall asleep during these meetings, or act in any way as if you think they're a joke.
- Attack the mediator.

Directly or indirectly, judges may hear about what happened in mediation, and it can have a profound effect on their decisions. Much of what takes place during mediation is supposed to be confidential. In reality, however, a significant amount of information may get back to the judge. If, for instance, a therapeutic mediator hears something during a mediation session that seems abusive to a child, he or she, as a mandated reporter, is required to report this suspicion to a governmental agency, such as the Department of Children and Family Services.

Consistency

Once the divorce is final, custody has been set, and visitation schedules have been nailed down, the real work for divorced dads begins. Exhibiting consistent parenting behavior is a defining trait of good divorced dads. Consistency means showing up when you're supposed to show up at places and events that are meaningful for your children. It also means that you're emotionally present when you do show up. Consistency is crucial for the well-being of your kids, especially if they're young. They need to rely on your being a regular part of their lives because it provides them a sense of security and stability that is crucial, especially in the wake of a divorce. If you aren't there, they may very well blame themselves for your absence—consciously or not. They will think they did something to drive you away. Even if you get it together at some later point in their lives, the damage will have been done. Child psychologists talk about attachment theory and how children must bond with their parents in order to have an inner security; the foundation of feeling attached and the knowledge that they are loved provides them with the strength to grow and develop. They are less likely to get in trouble at school, do drugs, and act out and more likely to achieve in school, make friends, and stay within the normal boundaries of teenage behavior.

Your consistent behavior goes a long way toward helping them attach and feel loved. Some divorced dads think they're being consistent because they always pick up their kids for the weekend visit or the weekday night that they have them. "I never miss my child's soccer games," one of these dads says. He might never miss them, but he spends more than half the games he attends reading the newspaper or talking on his cell phone.

Similarly, some divorced dads believe they are being consistent because they are in physical proximity to their kids on a regular basis. Yet many of these dads are doing nothing more than warehousing them. In other words, when they have the kids, they plunk them down in front of the television, or they have their own friends over to play poker, or they fall asleep on the couch. Even worse, they hire someone to do the job they should be doing.

Affluent fathers who have high-powered professional jobs are most guilty of these counterproductive behaviors. Doctors, lawyers, business executives, and others sometimes hire babysitters and nannies or bring in their own parents or siblings to help care for the children while they're busy with work. They rationalize this behavior: "I have to pay exorbitant support and maintenance amounts, and I can't do it unless I work like a demon." When workaholicism gets in the way of being a consistently present parent, it's not worth it.

In fact, often the work is just an excuse. The divorce process can be so stressful and upsetting that even decent, caring men can become angry, confused, or self-hating and not think clearly. Their emotional pain is so intense that they don't even realize they are neglecting their children.

To help you move past your emotional pain and maintain a consistent relationship, here are some suggestions:

Do

- Treat your visitation schedule as sacred time. Unless you have a real emergency, adhere to it. Don't let work, a new girlfriend, or vacation get in the way.
- Make an effort to engage with your children. Engaging means talking to them, playing with them, and taking them places. It doesn't mean asking a few general questions and making some perfunctory remarks. Demonstrate to them that you're happy to be with them, that you want to know about their lives, and that you remember the things that are important to them.

- Attend events that are important to your child, even if these events may make you uncomfortable. Perhaps your ex-wife's new boyfriend will be at your child's school play. Maybe her parents will be there, and they hate you and blame you for the failure of the marriage. Maybe going to the school open house and sitting there talking to your child's teacher with your ex-wife right next to you causes you pain. Get over it! By being a regular, involved attendee at these events, you're communicating to your kids that you're not going to disappear from these key parts of their lives. You recognize the importance of the event to them, and you're going to do everything possible to attend them.

Don't

- Be present one week, absent the next. Even if you're feeling down about something or furious with your ex, rally! Don't allow a bad day at the office or a hateful comment from your ex cause you to be less than a present parent every other week.

- Rationalize why you shouldn't be with your kids on certain days. Don't tell yourself that you're under too much pressure and need a break from your children. Don't tell yourself that your children are in a bad mood and need a break from you. If you think about it, you'll realize that your responsibility to be a present parent trumps just about every rationalization.

Planning

Good dads plan, and dads who fall short of their parenting challenges wing it. If you're not the custodial parent, your time with your kids is limited, so make the most of it. If you don't plan, you're likely to just ask your kids what they want to do, and when they say they want to watch television or play video games or text their friends, you'll most likely say, "Fine," in order to make them happy. But you'll end up being an observer at best. Good divorced dads value their time and plan ahead to maximize that value. Don't become a Disneyland Daddy or Uncle Daddy.

You don't have to plan every moment of every day you spend with your children, but make sure that at least part of the time involves specific activities you've made an effort to arrange. These don't have to be elaborate or expensive activities. Trips to the zoo, a museum, or an athletic events are perfect. Take your kids on hikes or out to eat. Shop beforehand and cook a meal together. Buy some jigsaw puzzles you can do around a table or board games that are age appropriate.

None of this is particularly difficult unless you're devastated by the divorce. Some dads exit the divorce process in an enervated state. They can barely lift up the phone to call their children, let alone plan an activity. Planning requires effort—not a lot of effort, but more than some dads feel capable of mustering. If you feel this way, you need to seek help from a therapist, or a life coach, or a trusted friend. Someone needs to give you a push to plan.

Do

- Be proactive in your thinking about activities with your children.
- Focus on things to do that would be fun and meaningful for them.

Don't

- Leave everything to the last minute and end up doing nothing or engaging in passive activities with your children like watching television.
- Tell yourself that your kids really just want to sit around and decide you'll accommodate them.

Your Relationship with Your Ex-Wife

This is the one that often causes problems with fathers. They explain that it's impossible to deal in a civilized manner with their ex-wives; these women are out to destroy them, as evidenced by their infidelity, or their bad-mouthing dad in front of the kids, or their unwillingness to compromise on visitation, or something else.

Therefore, heed these do's and don'ts:

Do

- Treat your ex with respect, even if she is behaving badly. It may be that she is a hostile, destructive person, or it may be that she acts that way because of the crucible that the divorce process can become. The reason doesn't matter. What matters is that you figure out how to communicate with her in a way that isn't harmful to your children.

- Keep her up to date in terms of your plans with the children. If she feels out of the information loop, she's going to become angry. Tell her in advance if you intend to do something unusual with the kids when you have them, like going on a camping trip. You may dislike talking to your former wife for a variety of good reasons, but keeping her informed of what you plan to do will allay her fears and may make her easier to deal with.

- Maintain an emotionally neutral stance. Unless you feel your ex is somehow endangering your children physically or causing them serious psychological harm, keep your cool. Good divorced dads recognize that there are thousands of friction points in the relationship. If you are not conscious of this fact, one of you will rub the other the wrong way, and sparks will fly. Be courteous and reticent. If there is an issue that's important to talk about that might get heated, have the conversation in private.

- Maintaining this emotional neutrality will be especially difficult if ongoing legal issues exist. If she is petitioning the court for more financial support or you're requesting a reduction in support, if there's a clash over the visitation schedule or some other issue, the adversarial legal process can spill over to your personal life. As difficult as it may be, separate the legal from the personal. If your ex-spouse is furious about something that took place in court, blame your lawyer. If you're furious about something that took place in court, have your lawyer handle it.

Don't

- Turn little things into big things. Maybe their mother is five minutes late in bringing the children to your house and you explode at her in front of the kids when she arrives: "You're never on time! You never do what you say! This is why we're no longer married." Perhaps she makes a reference to your job relative to the more prestigious one of her new boyfriend. Maybe you forgot to talk to your accountant about some financial issues like you promised, and she reminds you again in front of the kids to talk to him. Whatever it is, don't turn her small, irritating comment or behavior into a big deal, especially in the presence of the children.

- Rehash old conflicts. Every marriage has its standard arguments—about money, other women or men, friendships, mothers-in-law. Just because the marriage ends doesn't mean that the arguments do too. It's easy to get pulled back into the old conflicts. If you argued about money during your marriage, the argument will likely resurface after you've been divorced. Maybe you can't buy your child the expensive video game he wants, and your ex-wife finds out and berates you in front of him. Don't let the old arguments escalate.

- Bad-mouth her in front of the children. It doesn't matter if she denigrates you in front of your son or daughter. Responding in kind makes it even worse for your children. Nonetheless, you're going to be sorely tempted to tear her down in their eyes, if only because of all negative things she's done to you or said about you. You may be tempted to blame her for the failure of the marriage, accuse her of sleeping around, suggest that your financial woes are her fault, imply that she's more interested in her career than her kids. Whenever there is any postdivorce stress, in fact, you may find yourself blaming your ex-wife and articulating that blame where the kids can hear. Do your best to avoid it.

Financial Support

Good divorced dads take their financial responsibilities to their children seriously. Dads who don't meet their parental challenges may use money as a tool. Most commonly, they send support checks late or for reduced amounts when they're angry at their ex-wife. In turn, the mom may threaten to withhold their visitation privileges unless they send money more than the amount ordered. The children get caught in the middle. Our legal system empowers custodial parents with visitation and noncustodial parents with money. If you're thinking about using this power because your ex is unfairly withholding visitation, remember that your support payments are for the kids. If you use financial support as a tool first, your wife is likely to respond in kind with her visitation power as a retaliatory strike. As a result, your kids won't get the money and they won't get to see you as much as they should. Neither you nor your spouse wins, and your kids are the biggest losers.

Another hot-button issue for divorced dads is a reduction in income. Larry lost his job shortly after his divorce and couldn't keep up with the support payments. Too embarrassed to tell his ex-wife that he was out of work, he scrambled to find part-time jobs that would help him meet his support payments. But this income wasn't sufficient for him to meet his obligations, so he reduced his support amount without telling his ex-wife he was doing so or why. When she confronted him, he lied and said that he had to make a major repair on his car that month, which was why he was short. But when he continued to send checks for a reduced amount the next two months, Larry's ex-wife became more and more angry. Their children were forced to skip some activities because Larry's ex-wife was on a tight budget too. The situation became increasingly tense, and Larry's ex-wife finally threatened to report him as a deadbeat dad to the court and have him thrown in jail.

At that point, he told her that he had lost his job and they managed to work things out until he found a new job a few months later, but the damage had been done. From that point on, the relationship between Larry and his ex-wife deteriorated, and they never trusted each other again. Worse, the kids witnessed the growing acrimony between them, which might all have been prevented.

If you find yourself in this difficult situation, here is some advice that will help you and your children:

Do

- Be up front with your wife about your inability to pay support. If you cannot make the required payments, petition the court for a reduction of support or an abatement (a temporary cessation of payments, typically when the dad has lost his job).

- Make sure the court, and not just your ex-wife, approves your reduction in support. Discussing the situation with your kids' mom is essential. In fact, you may have a very understanding ex-wife who will tell you that it's fine to reduce payments temporarily while you look for a new job or pay off a debt. But if the court does not sanction this reduction, then you may build up an arrearage that will have to be repaid or face jail time. There has been more than one case of a man who received his ex-wife's verbal okay for a reduction, and then five years later, she petitioned the court for payment of years of arrearages, claiming that she never gave him permission to reduce the payments.

- Overcome your depression, denial, or fear of the legal system. Maybe you become so depressed that you can't work, or you quit your job or are fired. You may be in denial about what your financial obligations are to your children, spending money you can't afford after the divorce. You may refuse to petition the court for a reduction in child support payments because your divorce case was traumatic and you fear returning to the legal system, even though you have a legitimate reason.

- Recognize that you are likely to encounter these barriers and resolve to get past them. You need to fight through your depression, face reality, and understand that the legal system can work for you, not just against you. Always keep in mind that it's worth the effort to work through your angst in therapy or on your own and seek out justice in the legal system so you don't end up a target.

Don't

- Request a reduction in financial support if you're financially able to pay the designated amount easily. This may seem like an obvious bit of advice, but some men, out of anger at their ex-wives or because the system took advantage of them, seek ways to reduce payments. Perhaps they quit their jobs, and they have managed to store away a lot of money. Or perhaps they quit their job and can obtain a new one relatively easily but fail to do so, telling themselves that they can make reduced payments as long as they don't have a job. Good divorced dads don't do these things. Not only can this hurt your kids and yourself, but the legal system usually is vigilant for this type of action. The court may look at your assets and determine if a reduction is warranted based on those assets. It may also hold you accountable for looking for a job. You may be required to keep a diary of your job search and report regularly to the court about that search. And if you don't have any income and are receiving unemployment insurance, the court will take a percentage of that unemployment compensation as support. Finally, if you left your job voluntarily, the court may interpret that action as an effort to avoid paying child support.

Communication

Good divorced dads communicate; dads who are physically or emotionally absent don't. More specifically, fathers who make an effort to communicate with their offspring are the ones who communicate their feelings; they're also the ones who listen actively and respond to what their children are feeling.

In a marriage, mom and dad typically assume gender-specific roles. Moms empathize; dads direct. If you doubt this generalization, think about what happened when you were a boy playing sports. If you or another boy was injured playing football or basketball, did everyone gather around the injured player, hug him, and ask how he was? No, of course not. But if you've observed girls playing soccer or other sports, that's exactly what they do. They're socialized to express feelings and listen deeply. Boys are socialized to be strong and hide feelings.

Gender-specific roles might work during a marriage, but after a divorce, if dad doesn't communicate well, his relationship with his kids suffers. The dynamic has changed, and his role should also shift. Kids can't talk to distant, cold divorced fathers. They have a relatively small window of time in which to communicate their joys and fears, and if dad doesn't seem open to that communication, the bond between them frays. The John Wayne role model doesn't work for divorced dads.

Do

- Transcend your traditional societal role. You don't have to be all touchy-feely, but you do have to be conscious of your tendency to cover up your feelings when you feel hurt. If, for example, your son tells you he invited his stepdad to his Little League game, let him know, without getting angry, that this upsets you and talk through it with him. Also avoid changing the subject when your kid brings up a difficult topic such as asking, "Are you going to get married again?"

- Practice active listening. I've seen a lot of dads who tune out when their children talk about something they're not interested in or who feel the need to dominate the discussion by talking about themselves. Bill was a classic example of this type of divorced dad. He was a highly successful corporate attorney with three children ages ten to fifteen, and when he was married, he used to entertain his kids with stories about work or about his minor league baseball career. He never paid much attention to his children except for how they did in sports and their grades. After the divorce, he felt that he was losing his connection with them. Although he adhered to his visitation schedule and went to all their significant school events, he found himself perplexed by them at times and wondering if they were the same kids he had known and loved when he was at home. One day, his youngest son told it to him straight when Bill asked about something his son thought he should have known: "You're not listening to me!" Bill decided that he would work, and work hard, at being a better listener. When his kids talked to him, he put down the newspaper, turned off the television or radio, and kept eye contact. He asked questions when they were done talking to make sure he understood what they were telling him. He also told them how he felt about what they had to say. All this serious listening paid dividends for Bill over time. Not only did his kids appreciate the effort he was making, but Bill found he was learning a lot more about his children than he had known when he was still married. Their relationship improved dramatically.

Don't

- Be the strong, silent type. Your children need you to engage with them consistently. The odds are that you want to engage, but you might be so upset with your ex that you find yourself furiously silent. Don't let your ex turn you into this unengaged stereotype.

- Hide your feelings. Instinctively, most men know that they need to forge an emotional bond with their children and not just a cognitive one. Don't be afraid to let your children see that you're sad or that you're happy. When you express your feelings, you're acting authentically, and children need that from their fathers.

Children's Emotional and Physical Health

Good divorced dads pay attention to what is happening with their kids, even when they're not directly in their care. They are alert for signs that problems exist: a naturally talkative child becomes unusually silent; unexplained bruises keep showing up on different parts of the child's body; acting out behavior, such as a child starts disrupting classes at school or engages in other acting-out behavior; the child starts showing lots of anger or other strong emotions.

You don't want to jump to false conclusions, but neither do you want to ignore signs that something is wrong. Therefore:

Do

- Pay attention to what you see and hear. Some dads notice but are afraid to say anything since they're intimidated by their ex-wife and don't want to get her riled up. Still others are uncomfortable discussing these emotional issues with their children, their ex, or anyone else.

- Be proactive. This might be nothing more than talking to your child about whatever problems she's experiencing. Perhaps a mean girl is picking on your daughter at school, making fun of the fact that she's a child of divorce, or it may be that she's being shunned by the popular kids for other reasons. Whatever the issue, recognize that you have as much right to talk to your daughter about it as her mom does. In fact, if you're more proactive than her mom, you may need to involve the child's mother in the conversation—she may have missed the signs you spotted—or bring in professional help. The keys are being watchful and taking action when it is called for.

- Your child may be the victim of neglect or physical or emotional abuse. Of course, you don't want to make inaccurate assumptions. Kids do fall down when they're playing and skin their knees; they get in fights with other kids and get black eyes. But if you suspect something more serious, you must take legal steps to protect your child. It may be that your son or daughter is suffering from neglect because their mother isn't taking care of them properly, or she could be abusing them or have a boyfriend who is abusing them.

- If your ex-wife has a boyfriend who seems to have problems—anger management, drugs, drinking—then you should be especially vigilant. In his book *Fatherless America*, David Blankenhorn notes, "What magnifies the risk for sexual abuse of children is not the presence of a married father but his absence."[1] Besides boyfriends, stepfathers, uncles, and other men may spend a significant amount of time alone with your child. Because you're not around and because they may have deceived the child's mom into trusting them (or intimidating her), they may have free rein to be abusive.

- Contact your attorney immediately and obtain an emergency order of protection if you believe sexual or physical abuse is occurring. Typically these orders are good for only a short period of time (for example, up to twenty-one days in Illinois). Although you may be successful in removing your child from a harmful environment and extending the order, you need to act quickly to keep him or her out of that environment. One of the most common—and sometimes tragic—mistakes that dads make is not gathering their evidence swiftly so they can present a convincing argument in court. During that window of time when the order of protection is in effect, you may need to put your child in therapy with an experienced, gender-neutral therapist (to help your child heal as well as to gather evidence of the abuse for the court), seek witnesses to the abuse who might testify, and so on. The worst thing you can do is remove the child from the abusive environment with a court order, anger the predator, not prepare for court, and then be forced by law to return the child to this abusive environment, where things are likely to get worse rather than better. Emotional abuse and neglect can be more difficult to prove, though if you believe it is occurring, a legal process exists to ascertain if the child is in danger. A parent who believes the other is guilty of this kind of abuse or neglect must follow a series of steps that your lawyer will outline for you. Typically nonbinding mediation and seeing a therapist are often part of the process. Some courts are not willing to hear a case until the parent has gone through these steps.

Don't

- Fabricate charges of abuse or neglect. Most divorced dads would never do anything like this, but I just want to emphasize what you probably already know: this is the wrong thing to do. Seeking vengeance through these charges will ultimately hurt the kids. Your ex-wife will be understandably outraged if you use these charges to seek vengeance (as you would be if the situation were reversed), and it will likely create such hostility that the two of you won't be able to be civil to each other in the presence of your children.

- Assume that your ex will protect your children from a boyfriend. She may not know that he's being abusive, or she may know and tell herself that he's assuming the role of father and is entitled to spank the children or punish them in other ways if they misbehave. Again, the majority of moms will protect their kids against any threat, but you should not assume this is the case. Be observant and talk to your children constantly. It's quite possible they'll say or do something that lets you know you need to intervene through your attorney.

Is It Easier to Be a Good Divorced Dad in Certain States?

This question might have occurred to you as you have been reading this chapter. You might think that one state is more likely to grant you custody or that the laws are more gender neutral or that they have more realistic child support guidelines. Variations certainly exist in divorce laws among the states, and their impact on whether you can protect your legal rights as a dad and meet your responsibilities must be known by your lawyer.

What can really matter is the judge who hears your case. Most judges are fair and unbiased, but a minority of judges are gender biased. I know of one judge who believes that when sex abuse charges are brought against dads, he should presume guilt; another judge was abused by his father as a child and has a strong bias against men; a third judge believes that mothers are almost always better parents than dads, and her custody rulings reflect this prejudice. If you are unfortunate enough to have a judge like this, you're likely to leave court angry at your ex-wife and unable to see your children as often as you want and as you should. In certain instances, your lawyer can request a different judge, so you should look for an attorney who knows the judges well.

Nonetheless, even if you have the misfortune of landing a gender-biased judge, you can still be a good divorced dad. If you understand the challenges when it comes to the issues addressed in this chapter—mediation, a relationship with your child's mom, and communication, for example—then you can make the right choices for yourself and your children.

CHAPTER 3

The Impact of Divorce on Children

The Knowledge You Need, the Actions You Should Take

In the previous chapter, you may have noticed that one trait of good divorced dads is paying attention to their child's emotional and physical health. This may seem like an obvious responsibility for all parents, but after a divorce, it becomes especially important. Divorce can have a huge impact on a child's well-being. The legal process and its aftermath can touch everything from how a child bonds with a parent, to her self-esteem, to her school performance. Sometimes the impact is obvious—a child starts acting out and getting in trouble after his parents go through a contentious divorce. Sometimes the impact is subtle: a child gradually becomes less communicative with one or both parents after her dad moves out of the house.

Divorced dads need to be keenly observant of their children's behaviors, they must know the psychological impact of divorce on kids of various ages, and they must understand what to do if they observe a negative impact. This chapter will help you gain this knowledge, but what's most important for you to do is to pay attention. It's too easy to be oblivious to, minimize, or rationalize the impact of divorce on kids, as the following story illustrates.

Stressed Out at Fifteen Years Old

Laura's parents were divorced when she was in eighth grade. The divorce was relatively amicable, but it nevertheless took Laura by surprise. When her dad moved out, she was shocked. She hadn't realized that her parents were having problems, and the announcement that they were getting divorced seemed to come out of the blue. Laura was reluctant to ask the questions about the divorce that were bothering her, so she never broached the subject with her mom or dad. For their part, Laura's parents never talked about the divorce with her or tried to anticipate her concerns and address them.

As a high school freshman, Laura received significantly poorer grades than she had in eighth grade. Just as telling, she became quieter and spent more time alone than with friends. She had been taking piano lessons since she was eight years old, and she was very good at it and seemed to like it. But she told her mother that she wanted to quit—she claimed she had lost interest in piano. Laura's parents discussed the matter and agreed to let her drop the lessons.

Although her parents were concerned about these changes, they didn't think they were of any great significance. Then Laura developed an eating disorder. In a matter of months, Laura, who was slender to begin with, lost over twenty pounds. Like many other anorexics, she was in denial about the eating disorder, claiming that she was trying to eat healthier, that she was exercising more.

When Laura started therapy and the therapist had her parents participate in some of the sessions, they learned that Laura was under extreme stress, largely caused by the divorce. Part of the stress was her fear that she was in part responsible for the divorce—that her parents' arguments over money often related directly to her (buying her clothes, paying for school trips). In fact, it turned out that the real reason she decided to stop taking piano lessons was that she wanted to save her parents' money. Another cause of the stress was Laura's worries about the future—she thought the divorce meant that she wouldn't be able to go on the trip to Europe with her school's French class and that she might not be able to afford college.

Although there's no guarantee that any of Laura's problems could have been avoided even if her parents had remained married, it's likely that divorce exacerbated the problems. Even worse, Laura's parents never were open and communicative about the divorce. They also never provided Laura with the opportunity to ask questions about her concerns or reassured her about their love and support for her despite the divorce.

Divorce puts a lot of stress on kids, especially adolescents like Laura, but parents can do a great deal to lessen that stress. As a good divorced dad, you need to be observant about stress-related behaviors as well as other likely reactions to the end of your marriage and beyond. Let's look at some of the common reactions by age group, since, as you'll discover, the impact of divorce affects children differently, depending on their age.

How Divorce Affects Four Age Groups

Obviously divorce can affect each child differently depending on his or her personality and circumstances. A child with low self-esteem may be even more devastated by her parents' divorce than a more inherently confident child. Kids who are thrown from a relatively stable home environment into a chaotic one because of the divorce may become more depressed or angry than other children in more secure environments. I've seen some children of clients weather the divorce process with few negative outward signs and others struggle mightily to cope with it. So to a certain extent, responses to divorce are highly individualized. At the same time, however, we can make accurate generalizations about how kids respond to divorce based on their age. Here are four age groups and the typical impact of divorce on each.

Ages Five and Under

Research indicates that divorce can affect children who are as young as two years old—and perhaps even those who are younger. Although toddlers aren't aware of what divorce means, studies have shown that they sense when a bond is being broken or diminished in some way; they recognize that their daddy isn't around as much as he used to be. From a psychological standpoint, they experience rejection when they should be experiencing attachment. It's difficult to know exactly what impact this has down the road, but psychologists speculate that it contributes to a variety of problems and disorders.

What we do know with greater certainty is how three- to five-year-old children are affected. They are most susceptible to the fear divorce creates—fear of who will take care of them, of the new boyfriend or girlfriend who may enter a parent's life, and so on. This is an age when children believe in monsters. They hear a noise in the closet, and they are convinced a demon is hiding there, and shadows on the wall at night appear to be living, menacing beings. Divorce amplifies this foreboding. Kids can respond to their fear by becoming overly timid or overly aggressive. Their toilet training can be affected by this fear, and they may experience difficulty sleeping.

In addition, some children in this age range become confused by divorce. The very idea of a mommy and daddy splitting up doesn't compute. As a result, they may start asking and repeating questions related to the split, for example, "Where's Daddy? Why isn't he here anymore?"

Ages Six to Nine

These kids possess some understanding of what divorce means. Because of this understanding, they often experience what psychologists term a loyalty conflict. In other words, they are torn between loyalty to one parent versus the other. This conflict can manifest itself in different ways. For instance, when moms become custodial parents of boys, these kids tend to be aggressive toward their mothers; consciously or not, they feel as if they have been forced to choose the mom's side and have betrayed their dad by doing so.

In a joint custody arrangement, kids often feel as if they're balanced precariously between mom and dad, and they may be reluctant to report any negative events that take place in either parent's house. For instance, it may be that mom's boyfriend does a lot of drinking and driving, and the child won't want to alienate his mom by telling his dad (or anyone else) about it. Or they have a great time with their dad and feel they're betraying mom in some way. No matter what they do, they're likely to feel disloyal. When a parent encourages his child to believe he's having more fun with him than her, they make this loyalty conflict more acute: "I'll bet your mom never lets you have ice cream for dinner like I do."

Ages Ten to Twelve

Their greater maturity helps these children grasp more about the divorce: they often understand the reasons that it took place. But kids in this age group are also more likely to be embarrassed by the divorce or resent it. Although they are better able than younger children at keeping their reactions to the divorce under control, they may have unpleasant dreams about the divorce or have other experiences that are unconscious reactions to their mom and dad splitting up.

This is also the time when kids have trouble controlling their emotions, and they may react angrily. Sometimes they express this anger to their mom or dad, but more often, they become angry at school. Some kids control their emotions at home, but at school they may get in fights with other kids or talk back to teachers. Acting out and other behavioral changes are common among kids in this age range after a divorce.

Ages Thirteen to Eighteen

Divorce can hit adolescents hard, even though they may seem mature enough to handle it like adults. In our society, however, teenagers struggle with many issues, and adjusting to a divorce may be one struggle too many. They are in the process of developing their identities, and divorce can hamper that process.

Although teenagers may not articulate their worries, their minds are often racing with disturbing questions: Will I ever see Dad again? Will Dad still coach my baseball team or even have time to play catch with me again? Will he come to my events at school if Mom is also attending? They also may question their own ability to get along with the opposite sex and wonder if they will ever want to get married.

Similar to younger tweens, teenagers may become angry in response to the divorce. They may also feel stressed by the process, their grades may drop, and they may turn to drinking and drugs to relieve the stress they feel.

What to Do: Responding to Kids in Ways That Help Rather Than Hurt

Knowing the previous information is crucial, but your mood and circumstances may be such that it's difficult to put this information to use on behalf of your child. In other words, you're so furious at the child's mom or you're in such precarious financial straits that helping your child through his or her struggles is not a priority for you. Perhaps you don't respond to your son's anger or your daughter's sudden drop in grades. Rather than seeing their changing behavior as signs you need to respond to, you can't see them because of your own problems.

Although it's difficult, you must put your child's problems first and your own second. No matter how depressed or angry or confused you are because of the divorce, get past your own issues and look at what your children are dealing with. Your kids need you and are vulnerable because of the divorce, and you need to be conscious about protecting them. When my clients are in the midst of the divorce process, they're often focused on the details of the divorce agreement: who gets what, what visitation will be, and so on. But once that agreement is finalized, they have more time and emotional space to consider issues beyond the nitty-gritty divorce issues. If you find yourself unable to focus on anything but the divorce details while you're going through it, resolve to focus on your kids as soon as possible.

When you are able to put your children's needs at the forefront, here are the steps you should take.

Respond in Age-Targeted Ways to Your Kids

The distinctions by age group at the start of this chapter are important; they provide clues about what to watch for in terms of your kids' reactions to the divorce and what they need from you. Very young children, for instance, don't require you to talk to them about the divorce in concrete term. Explaining why you and their mom are no longer together isn't something they're capable of grasping. What they do require from you, however, is reassurance. You have to foster a sense of security and safety in their minds, and you can do that by communicating clearly and regularly that you'll be there for them no matter what happens.

In the initial stages of the divorce, tell these young children that they're not losing you or their mommy. When your child expresses a fear, respond to it. Don't lie to your child and say that everything is going to be the same, especially if you're the noncustodial parent. You have to be honest and talk about how you won't be living with him (if that's the case) and that you're going to see him only on certain days and at certain times. But you can also talk to your child about how you're going to see him regularly: you're still going to take him to the park and make his favorite sandwich and do all the other things you did in the past. It may seem like a small thing, but to a small child, these words are tremendously reassuring.

For the next age group, ages six to nine, make an effort to avoid creating or exacerbating the loyalty conflict. Don't pit yourself against your ex-wife and make your kids choose sides. Don't ask: "Do you want to sit with me or your mom at your cousin's wedding?" Don't make them feel guilty for living with their mom or because they have to go to a stepsibling's event rather than do something with you. Instead, make an effort to use *we* when talking about yourself and your ex-spouse: "We think it's best if you go to bed at nine during the week." Do everything possible to avoid communicating your animosity toward your ex or the belief that she's doing something wrong as a parent.

For kids ages ten to twelve, be alert and responsive to displays of anger, embarrassment, or resentment. If they seem to be exhibiting these behaviors more frequently or more intensely than before the divorce, make an effort to talk with them about it in a nonjudgmental way. Focus on their specific behaviors: yelling at a sibling, speaking disrespectfully to you or your ex, not wanting to be seen in public with you. Let your child vent. She needs to express her feelings directly to you and her mom. Be aware, too, that some kids this age won't express these emotions at home but will act out in school, where it feels safer for them to do so. Again, engage them in conversations about what took place, and let them speak about their feelings.

For teenagers, try to relieve some of the pressure they feel to deal with the divorce. Recognize the types of stress they may feel because of your failed marriage and encourage them to share with you why they feel stressed. They may worry about who's going to teach them to drive, pay for college, and give them advice when they need it. They may feel they were in part responsible for the divorce (financially or otherwise). Make sure they understand they are not responsible for any of this and that you and their mom will support them just as you were there when you were married. Tell them to pay attention to the things they should be focusing on: schoolwork, friends, dates, learning to drive.

Spend More Time with Your Kids

Your divorce settlement entitles you to a certain number of hours with your child if you're the noncustodial parent, so don't miss a minute of that time. And as I suggested earlier, capitalize on opportunities to add to these hours.

It's especially important to spend time with younger children at bedtime. Bonding between parent and child takes place in part on an unconscious level. For instance, psychologists will tell you that when a parent puts a child to bed—reading him a story, saying a prayer with him, tucking him in before he goes to sleep—these actions reduce that child's anxiety. Studies have shown that kids have fewer nightmares and sleep more soundly when parents participate in their bedtime rituals. A number of our clients have worked out agreements with their kids' moms to come over to the house at least one additional time (beyond what's in the parenting order) weekly to sit with the child before he goes to sleep.

Bring In an Outside Professional If You See Alarming Signs

Don't leave this responsibility to the child's mom, even if she is the custodial parent. You may notice things she does not. If you observe or hear about a behavior that strikes you as a red flag, talk to her about it and make a plan to bring in a professional to help.

You may see significant changes in behavior (a talkative child may suddenly seem unusually quiet, or she may now say she dislikes an activity she formerly liked); changes in eating habits, especially loss of weight; falling grades; getting in fights with another child at school; loss of friendships; bedwetting; night terrors; or a significant increase in anger and hostility.

Obviously you don't want to overreact to one or two incidents. A single bedwetting incident isn't cause for alarm; neither are one or two angry arguments or a bad grade in one subject. It's only when you start seeing a pattern develop in any of the problem areas that you need to take action.

This can mean bringing in a qualified therapist to talk with you, your ex, and your child and begin regular therapy sessions if necessary. But it doesn't have to be a psychologist or other traditional therapist. It can be clergy, a guidance counselor at school, a favorite teacher, or a coach. You need to use your judgment as to who is in the best position to help your child deal with a specific problem. What is key is to recognize when there is a problem and to take action sooner rather than later (or not at all).

The Legal System and Kids: Managing the Interaction

The legal process can be traumatic or therapeutic for kids depending on how it is used. Good divorced dads recognize that they are not always at the mercy of the process. They understand the positive and negative ways the legal aspects of a divorce can affect their children, and they opt for legal strategies that never hurt their children and sometimes even help them. All you need is a little bit of knowledge about the legal system to minimize the damage it can do to your child.

First, and most obvious, keep your children out of court if possible. Because most judges, lawyers, and parents recognize that having kids testify generally isn't a good idea, it's far less common now than it used to be. Nevertheless, some people are so angry at their spouse and so intent on vengeance that they will insist to their lawyers that the kids testify about their spouse's bad behavior. Don't succumb to this impulse, no matter how you feel. Younger kids especially should not be asked to speak negatively about one parent or to be subjected to cross-examination, no matter how gentle you are told it might be. In addition, most children associate courts with criminal behavior, so they may believe that either of their parents have done something wrong. Although there are exceptions to this guideline—a child's testimony may be necessary to remove him from a physically abusive environment—most of the time you should do everything possible to keep your kids out of court.

This also means you should keep them out of the courtroom even if they're not testifying. There is no positive outcome to having your kids witness your lawyer and your wife's lawyer slugging it out and hearing them speaking negatively about each of you. Similarly, don't talk to your kids about the specific charges and countercharges, negotiating points, and conflicts surrounding the divorce. Your child doesn't need to know why your wife is insisting on supervised visitation or why you believe she won't spend the time necessary to be a good custodial parent. If your child asks a question about the divorce, you can talk about the process in neutral terms and, of course, explain what the settlement means for your child in terms of custody and visitation. What you don't want to do is enmesh your kid in the vituperative aspects of the divorce.

Third, choose attorneys who do more than just give lip-service to arguments focusing on the best interests of the child. Some attorneys relish divorce warfare, knowing that the more fighting that occurs between spouses, the more legal fees they will receive. Other attorneys are combative by nature and believe in attacking first and compromising second. They may have good intentions—they want the best settlements for their clients—but they exact a price that's generally not worth paying. Parents who are "beaten up" by aggressive attorneys during the divorce process can bear the scars long after the divorce is final. This is especially true for dads. When they are castigated for not earning enough money, failing to attend key events in their child's life, being verbally abusive, and for countless other things, they often emerge from the divorce with low self-esteem. They may believe they aren't good people or good parents and feel their kids would be better off without their being a consistent presence in their lives. You don't want your lawyer to have this effect on your wife, and you don't want her lawyer to have this effect on you. Be aware that if you hire a cutthroat lawyer, your wife is likely to respond in kind, and so you'll both be demeaned in the process and cut each other's throat.

Fourth, the best legal strategy may not be the best strategy psychologically for your children. It may be in your best financial interest to hire a private investigator to tail your wife and document her extravagant spending or to demand sole custody because you know something incriminating about her from the past (and threaten to reveal it in court), but pursuing these and other courses of action may harm your kids directly or indirectly. This must be analyzed on a case-by-case basis.

If you believe your wife is a good mom, then you should not do anything that would make her a worse mom after the divorce. If you demean her or rob her of the chance to be a coequal parent, you're not doing your kids any favors. I'm not suggesting you give your wife everything she's asking for or refuse to battle for what's fair, but you may need to find a compromise between the optimum legal approach and the optimum approach for your kids' well-being. For example, if you believe that one parent should stay home with the kids until they reach a certain age and you're not able to be there, don't force her to go back to work. If you can financially swing it for a few years, allow her to stay home if you believe it will benefit your children.

Custody Arrangements to Suit Your Kids

Joint custody or joint parenting is usually the best outcome of divorce. Psychologists have talked and written about the importance to children of divorce of having both parents actively involved in their lives, and my observations of thousands of children have confirmed this finding. The kids whose parents are deeply involved in their lives generally flourish, while those where only one parent (or neither parent) is involved are more likely to experience problems.

That said, let me issue a few words of warning about joint custody. It may describe your legal situation but not your reality. In some instances, dads may have joint custody but they don't take full advantage of it, instead ceding all decision-making authority to their ex-wives and not participating in other parenting activities. In other instances, their ex-wives manipulate the situation to deny them equal parenting status. And there are joint custody agreements that are impossible to enforce: dads might have equal parenting rights under the law, for example, but they may live too far away to see their kids regularly and participate in key activities.

Obviously you want to do everything possible so that you are a coparent not just in legal terms but in fact. This means trying to live geographically close so you can take advantage of your rights, and it means taking full advantage of your rights to be with your child rather than exercising these rights inconsistently.

Perhaps the most important issue for divorced dads is making sure the custody agreement is tailored to their specific situation. The language of the agreement must take into consideration the geographical location of both parents, their work schedules, educational issues, health issues, and many others. Anticipate the subjects and decisions that might cause you and your ex to argue about, and try to include provisions within the agreement that will mitigate or resolve arguments. For example, you can specify that you're to be informed of and participate in every parent-teacher conference, attend every school concert or play, and pick up your child from school every Friday. Agreements that detail these issues help men be good divorced dads; they put your rights in writing and decrease the odds that you'll be left out of the parenting loop inadvertently or on purpose.

You also should insist on language in the agreement that protects your child from known dangers or at least provides preventative measures for potentially dangerous situations. For instance, if you know that your wife's father drinks a lot and sometimes drives after a few drinks, you can insert language in the agreement that she can't allow her father to drive your child anywhere. Many men don't realize that they can include such specific measures in agreements that protect their children in this way.

It is important to include a clause in custody agreements about mandatory mediation when parental conflicts occur. You may balk at such a clause, since when the agreement is being constructed, you probably are fed up with anything having to do with the seemingly endless legal hoops you have to jump through to finalize the divorce. Yet this clause can help dads when the moms, who often are the custodial parents, try to manipulate this situation to their advantage after the divorce is finalized.

Tammy had custody of eight-year-old Joey. According to the agreement, her ex, Tom, was entitled to talk to Joey on the phone every day when he didn't have visitation. When Tom remarried, Tammy was incensed; in fact, she had clung to the hope that she and Tom might get back together despite the divorce. When this hope was dashed, Tammy looked for small ways to get back at Tom, and one tactic was telling him that he could call Joey only between 7:00 and 8:00 P.M. on weeknights. This was also the only hour that Tammy allowed Joey to watch television, and so Tom's call came at the precise moment when Joey was least interested in talking to anyone. Joey was distracted during the calls, and Tom found them unsatisfying because Joey clearly wasn't engaged. But because of the mandatory mediation clause in the agreement, Tammy was not able to get away with this manipulative tactic. Tom exercised this clause, and Tom and Tammy then met with an exceptional mediator—an individual who not only was a skilled facilitator and had high emotional intelligence but was also gender neutral. As a result of working with the mediator, they settled this dispute outside court; Tammy stopped interfering with the telephone contact.

Observe Your Children Closely

Good divorced dads recognize that divorce can affect their kids in many ways, and so they pay attention to what their children do and say, and they are alert to indications that their children are having difficulty coping with the end of their parents' marriage. They're especially alert for significant behavioral changes—mood swings, eating disorders, falling school grades. Above all else, they don't fool themselves into believing that their kids are immune to the psychological impact of a divorce.

To prevent yourself from falling into this trap, consider the following conclusions of studies on divorce and kids:

- "Children who experience parental divorce, compared with children in continuously intact two-parent families, exhibit more conduct problems, more symptoms of psychological maladjustment, lower academic achievement, more social difficulties and poorer self-concepts."[1]
- "Following divorce, boys often display poorer academic adjustment as well as hostility, antisocial behavior, aggressions and depression."[2]
- "In a sample of ethnically diverse 11–14 year-olds of divorced and married parents, it was found that children of divorce had significantly more substance-using friends and [were] less likely to use effective coping and social skills."[3]

More specifically, pay attention to what your kids are saying and doing after the divorce by asking yourself these questions:

- Do they seem unusually hostile? Do they have more temper tantrums than in the past? Does their anger seem to be out of proportion to whatever causes it?
- Have you noticed that they become uncharacteristically silent for periods of time?
- Do they seem to be losing self-confidence? Are they unwilling to try things because they're afraid of failing? Do they talk negatively about their abilities frequently?
- Are they receiving significantly lower grades than in the past?
- Have you or someone else caught them using drugs or drinking? Do they exhibit some of the classic signs of drinking and drug use?
- Does it seems as if your children are stressed out? Depending on their age, signs of stress can manifest themselves as bedwetting, digestive ailments, headaches, trouble sleeping, or nightmares.
- Are they getting in more trouble than in the past at school? Are they receiving detentions and suspensions?

If you observe any of these behaviors, you need to address them directly or indirectly. If the problems are persistent and serious, you need to bring in a professional. In the majority of cases, though, the key is communicating honestly and consistently with your child and providing the reassurance he or she craves. More than anything else, kids need to believe that you are there for them now and will be there for them in the future. You can provide this reassurance through words and deeds. Talk about how you're always going to be part of their lives and that you will continue doing things like attending their concerts, picking them up from school on Fridays, taking them to their dentist appointments, and going camping with them. Don't miss any scheduled dates with your kids, and plan things to do together in the future.

Finally, don't go overboard and make promises you can't keep. Some dads feel so guilty about the divorce that they'll do anything to try to cheer up their children. One of the most common mistakes in this regard is leading kids to believe that you and your ex might get back together. A daughter might tell you that it seems as if you and her mom are getting along well; then she might ask if you like her mom more now than you did when you both were fighting all the time.

Most dads are tempted to answer this question affirmatively without broaching the subject of remarriage. They want to make their kids happy. That's fine, except that in the process of cheering up your child, you're also encouraging a fantasy. The vast majority of divorced couples don't remarry each other, and kids need to confront this reality. Consider how traumatic the divorce was in the first place. You want to help them get past that trauma, not have to experience it all over again. So level with your children. Explain that you respect, and perhaps even like or admire, their mom, but that you both function better as friends than as a married couple, and to keep this relationship healthy, you need to keep things as they are. Obviously how you convey this message depends on the age of your children, but the point is to make sure they understand that you and their mom are not going to remarry if that is not a possibility.

Turn a Negative into a Positive

For all the negative effects of divorce on children in the short term, it doesn't have to become a negative in the long term. In fact, some kids breathe a sigh of relief when parents divorce, even though they wish they could have found a way to stay together. Kids suffer when their mom and dad fight constantly. Witnessing one parent verbally abusing another or both abusing each other is tough for children to witness. If there's physical abuse, it's even more difficult. The divorce, by removing one parent from the household, also can make daily life calmer for kids. Ideally, the conflict between the parents diminishes over time and children aren't stressed out by continuous battles.

Beyond this immediate benefit, an opportunity exists to be a better parent to the child after divorce than during a marriage. Many dads may have withdrawn from the household because of the disintegrating relationships with their spouse; they may have spent as much time as possible at work, traveling, or with friends so they weren't physically present for their children.

I've seen how divorce can wake up dads to their responsibilities as parents. When they no longer have unlimited access to or time with their children, they begin to take being a father seriously. They go to their children's events that they never attended in the past. They listen more intently to what their sons and daughters have to say. They schedule activities that allow them to engage with their kids rather than lie on the couch and watch television.

If you take advantage of this opportunity, you can create a better relationship with your kids after the divorce than you had before. This will benefit their development and, ideally, offset at least some of the negative psychological effects of the divorce.

CHAPTER 4

Romance

Use Your Head When It Comes to Your Heart

Someone once said that love makes fools of us all, and that statement is especially applicable to divorced dads and moms. In the wake of a divorce, both men and women may see a new romantic relationship as an opportunity for vengeance and control. For instance, a man seeks a new partner in order to assert his masculinity and demonstrate to his ex that he is still "a catch"; or a woman seeks a new partner to provoke her ex, make him jealous, throw it in his face that his kids really like the new guy in her life.

New romantic relationships can be devastating in many different ways for children. A new romance can create divided loyalties, a subject I touched on in the previous chapter. It can expose kids to new men who may be verbally, physically, or sexually abusive. And it can ratchet up the level of tension between their mom and dad, resulting in all sorts of internecine warfare in which the children are the primary victims.

Good divorced dads recognize the potential fallout of new relationships for both themselves and their ex-wives, and they do whatever is necessary to protect their children. Admittedly this can be a challenge at times. Jim, a father of two small children, was going through a divorce when he met Tina. Almost instantly, they fell in love, recognizing that they were meant to be together. But there were problems. For one thing, Jim's wife, Jenny, was furious that he had decided to end the marriage. As soon as she learned about Tina, she began threatening to fight him on joint custody and insisting on supervised visitation. Jim knew that he would have a much easier time achieving a fair settlement if he stopped seeing Tina until the divorce was final, but that was easier said than done. Tina wanted him to move in with her. She was jealous of Jenny and worried that Jim might go back to her. So she was putting pressure on Jim to make a commitment.

Although Jim finally found a good compromise position—he suspended the relationship with Tina for the course of the divorce and promised to move in with her once the divorce was final— he was terrified of losing Tina and considered moving in with her immediately. Fortunately, he and his lawyer talked about what would be in the best interest of his kids, and it became clear that their interests were best served by waiting until after the divorce to make this move.

Romance, then, can pose a variety of problems and conundrums for divorced dads. One of the most common issues is starting another relationship before the current one is legally over. If you or your wife does this—or if either of you does it the wrong way—your kids will suffer. Here's what you need to know to protect your children in these situations.

Be Patient and Discreet

The divorce process can drag on for weeks or months or even years. During this time, you need to be on your best behavior, not just for yourself but for your children. Remember that your goal is to obtain a settlement that allows you to be as present as possible in your children's lives. Therefore, the last thing you want to do is make the process longer, more complex, or more confrontational. All of these are likely to happen if you flaunt your relationship with another woman before the agreement is signed.

For your own sake as well as the sake of your kids, then, follow these guidelines.

Don't Try to Make Your Wife Jealous

Whether it's conscious or unconscious, don't try and get back at your wife through relationships with women, especially her best friend. This isn't a gender-based behavior; women do the same thing. But if you're a divorcing dad whose wife dumped you, you're going to be especially vulnerable to this kind of behavior. You're going to want to throw it in her face that you are still desirable to other women, even if you have no feelings for the other women who desire you.

Another related mistake is implying that you have a relationship with an attractive woman when you do not. Again, you might want to communicate that your wife has made a huge error in dumping you and that you still have a lot of appeal for women. In fact, I know of a number of divorcing dads who have hired attractive women lawyers primarily to irritate their wives. During negotiations, these men frequently touch their lawyers on the shoulder, whisper conspiratorially, and imply that there's more going on than the typical lawyer-client relationship.

You may succeed in making your wife jealous through these behaviors, but there's a significant legal cost: jealous moms will get back through any means at their disposal, and typically their weapons are the children. If you make your ex-wife sufficiently jealous—and furious—expect her to strike back by fighting you on custody and imposing unfair restrictions on your visitation. She may even become so jealous and angry that she'll make up accusations of abuse and domestic violence against you to prevent you from seeing your children as often as you should.

Wait; If You Can't Wait, Be Discreet

Ideally you won't start a new relationship until the divorce is final because aggravating your divorcing wife in any way during the settlement negotiations is a bad idea. In addition, if you start seeing someone before the divorce is final, your spouse could accuse you of "dissipating marital assets"—spending money on your new girlfriend that legally belongs to both of you. Typically men don't think about the implications of taking their new girlfriends to fancy restaurants or buying them gifts. But then their spouse gets wind of this; maybe dads even rub it in by mentioning they took these other women to their former favorite restaurant or someone sees them there and tells the spouses—and her lawyer begins collecting evidence of dissipation of assets.

Even more problematic is the impact these new relationships can have on children. Many kids, especially younger ones, aren't emotionally prepared to see their dad with another woman. It can be a traumatic experience, and therapists usually advise both men and women to wait until weeks or months after the divorce before introducing kids to the new man or woman in a parent's life. Keep in mind that you're divorcing your spouse, not the kids. This isn't just semantics. You may feel compelled to begin a new relationship immediately because your wife kicked you out of the house, but that relationship is going to have a huge psychological impact on most children. It's best to let them get used to the idea of the divorce and that you and their mom are no longer together.

If you're unable to wait, be discreet. Don't flaunt the new relationship. First and foremost, don't have your new girlfriend stay over at your house. In fact, this is often how the kids and your spouse discover the relationship (someone stops in unexpectedly or discovers evidence that another woman was there). Try to avoid purchasing anything significant for the new woman in your life, especially using a credit card. Stay out of public places. Limit the frequency with which you see her. Above all else, don't talk about this wonderful new relationship to friends and family members. Even if they promise to be discreet, the odds are that someone will tell someone else and your spouse may explode and want revenge. The tools of revenge are often the children.

Be Aware of Alienation of Affection

"Alienation of affection" refers to a lawsuit brought by one spouse against the other spouse's lover, claiming that this person was responsible for destroying the marriage. Although this isn't always easy to prove in court, the simple act of your wife's filing a lawsuit against your girlfriend can have negative consequences for you, your new girlfriend, and the children.

Let's say you've moved in with your girlfriend, and your wife hears from a mutual friend that the girlfriend convinced you to move out and in with her. Here is what is likely to happen:

- Your wife's attorney will depose your new girlfriend and subject her to a series of tough, potentially humiliating questions. He might ask her about how many other marriages she's ruined in the past, whether she is looking for financial gain in the relationship with you, and so on.
- Your wife will be so angry at you that she's likely to fabricate charges of abuse and domestic violence against you—both in court and to the children—that she would never make in ordinary circumstances.
- Your new girlfriend may become equally angry at being dragged into this legal predicament and incurring significant financial losses. She may become so upset that she leaves you.

Alienation of affection is a cause of action (that is, a civil lawsuit) that is unfamiliar to many people these days, including other lawyers. I once had a case where I was taking a deposition of my client's wife's lover and he bragged about his sexual prowess with my client's wife, denigrated my client's job and earning power, and mentioned that he had told the wife that he could provide a much better life for her and the children. During this deposition, my client's wife sat next to her lover laughing. Astonishingly, the opposing lawyer didn't warn him about saying these things or object to my pointed questions. At the time of this deposition, the settlement negotiations had bogged down and the wife was refusing to settle on terms that were fair. As soon as the deposition was concluded, I informed the wife's lover that he had just testified to committing alienation of affection; he had just provided irrefutable evidence of it and could likely expect a lawsuit. Needless to say, he was alarmed, and his alarm helped us settle the divorce on favorable terms to my client.

Bringing a New Person into Your Child's Life

Most divorced dads believe that once the divorce is over, they can resume dating without worry; they can enter into a relationship and even remarry and not be concerned about the impact on the ex or their children. If you're a good divorced dad, however, you recognize that postdivorce relationships can have a huge effect on your kids. In fact, you have to be alert for issues not only in your own new relationships but those of your ex.

Of course, your ex will be upset if you bring a negative influence into your children's lives. You're going to be alert to that negative influence and take steps to shield your kids from it. I'm assuming that you understand it's a bad idea to introduce your children to a woman who uses drugs, drinks to excess, or is physically and verbally abusive. In addition to being a bad thing for your children directly, if you don't protect your kids from this type of person, your ex will likely come after you through legal means. If you're the custodial parent, that can mean removing the kids from your care. If you're the noncustodial parent or have joint custody, it might mean placing severe restrictions on visitation; for example, your children may be forbidden to stay overnight at your house. In the worst case, you might not be allowed to see your children at all.

Ideally, the new person in your or your ex's life is a good human being who will treat your kids with kindness. Ideally, he or she won't bring things to the relationship that directly or indirectly have a negative effect on your children.

You can't take the chance, though, that everything is going to be ideal. And even if this new person is a decent human being, other factors can come into play that cause harm to your child. Therefore, good divorced dads do the following regarding new romantic relationships.

Consider lobbying for a clause in the settlement or joint custody agreement that prohibits either person from allowing an unrelated adult to stay overnight. The language varies—some agreements forbid cohabitation—but the goal is to prevent kids from experiencing mom or dad living with another person. This can be especially threatening to younger kids who see the new person as usurping the role of the mom or dad: "Is he going to be my new dad?" is a question many moms receive in this situation. Realistically, you, your spouse, or both of you may not want this clause in the agreement because you're already in a serious relationship and don't want to be prohibited from cohabitating or you don't want that restriction to hamper your future relationships. If you decide you don't want this clause in your agreement, you need to be aware that if you move in with someone or your ex does, it can create a tremendous amount of conflict. It may be that both you and your ex tell each other you are fine with them living with other people, but as we'll see, many different problems arise when people cohabitate.

When in Doubt, Check Them Out

This advice should be followed whether this person has moved in or is just a frequent visitor, and it goes for your romantic interest as well as your wife's. While this individual has more access to the kids if he or she is living with the custodial parent, he or she still will have interactions with the children that can be negative even if your wife or you and this person are just dating. If you have any doubt about your ex-wife's new guy or the woman you're dating, check them out for your children's sake.

This isn't as difficult to do as it might seem, and it can be done without their being aware you're doing it. Our firm retains a licensed private detective to do background checks for our clients, and certainly you can hire your own detective, but there are a number of simple things you can do on your own. A great deal of information is available on Web sites—many states have sites that list the names of child molesters or sex offenders. Similarly, you can do online searches, both free and ones you pay for, that can determine if an individual has ever served time or been convicted of a crime.

Observe, Listen to Your Children, and Tell Your Attorney If Anything Seems Wrong

Pay attention to what you see and hear. If you have the opportunity to interact with your ex's boyfriend, watch what he says and how he says it. Is there anything off about him? Does he seem overly secretive? Has your ex ever said anything to you about him that gives you pause? Perhaps she's mentioned he has a bad temper or doesn't have any friends. If you watch him with your kids, how does he seem? Does he pay attention to them, or does he ignore them completely? Is he considerate of their feelings, or does he order them around?

Be aware that you may jump to conclusions because you may automatically hate the person your former spouse is with and assume the worst about him. For this reason, you need to do two things if you have suspicions about the new person in your ex-wife's life. First, listen attentively to anything your children say that relates to this person, either directly or indirectly. If he's abusive or neglectful, they probably won't accuse him, especially if they're younger. Instead, they may start acting differently after they're around him for a while: they may seem much quieter, for example, or may start acting out. It's also possible that they'll say something about how he doesn't talk much, how he became angry about something, about how he shoved their mother.

One caveat: don't ask your children in an aggressive tone or manner what they think of this guy and what he's done wrong. This can cause a variety of problems, especially if he's innocent of any wrongdoing and it gets back to their mom. It also may cause them to tell you what you want to hear (in order to please you) rather than reflect what's really going on. For this reason, you need to listen attentively to your kids and watch for changes in their behaviors.

Second, talk to your attorney about what you've heard and observed. Many times, dads come into our office and say something to the effect of, "I'm kind of worried about my wife's new boyfriend, but I don't have any proof that he's doing anything wrong."

You don't need proof; your attorney's job is to gather that proof based on your suspicions. Divorce lawyers can use licensed private detectives and other means to ascertain if the new guy is a danger to your kids. Generally, though, where there's smoke there's fire. If your child told you that the boyfriend became enraged the other night and smashed his hand into the wall, then it may be that he has an anger management problem and might have a criminal record for aggravated battery; he might have been married before and his previous wife took out an order of protection against him. Whatever it is, your attorney should be able to investigate and find out if there's a problem that needs to be solved to protect your children.

What to Do Based on What You Discover

If you believe that your wife has started a relationship with someone whose behaviors concern you, what you should do depends on what these behaviors are.

Let's say you feel that the man she's moved in with or is seeing a lot poses a physical danger to your kids. Perhaps your wife or your children have told you that they're afraid of him or that he's struck them or threatened to hit them; perhaps you see that your children have bruises; perhaps you discover that he's an ex-con who did time for a violent crime. Whatever it is, you need to tell your lawyer and seek an emergency order of protection immediately without notice to the other side (ex parte). Essentially this means that your attorney requests an immediate court date to deal with this issue and the other side doesn't have to be given notice about it. The lawyer creates an affidavit based on what you've told him and then files an emergency petition for an order of protection with the affidavit. In some instances, the process of filing an emergency emotion—from the time the client tells the lawyer until the court orders the kids removed from danger—can take less than twenty-four hours. The process can take much longer if your lawyer doesn't prioritize your case or doesn't have the time to do so.

Even if the danger isn't physical, you can still file a petition to protect your children from verbal abuse, neglect, and other threats. If you think that your ex's new boyfriend is contributing to the neglect and emotional abuse of your child—that they go out and leave your young kids home alone, for example, and then come home and emotionally abuse them, for instance—that can be considered abuse under the Domestic Violence Act. You could be able to obtain emergency relief for removal of your children to your care in certain circumstances. This can result in a court-ordered intervention that leads to a number of actions: the court orders the mom to undergo counseling, for instance, or she agrees to cease the negative behavior that caused you to take legal action in the first place.

Supervision of the mother's visitation is also a common court response when you initiate this type of legal action. The court may determine that what is referred to as "therapeutic supervised visitation" is necessary; this means that her time with the children is supervised by a mental health professional. Sometimes, though, the court assigns a maternal relative or friend to supervise, and this often proves ineffective (either the supervisor is lax or your wife intimidates or ignores this friend or relative). Courts make this mistake for a number of reasons, but usually because they don't know the case well enough to realize that a friend or relative is inadequate in this role. When the court's language specifies therapeutic supervised visitation, however, that should ensure that a mental health professional will be involved.

Recognize, too, that the nonlegal remedy of talking to your ex and asking her to remove the boyfriend from the house or get him to stop yelling all the time is generally ineffective. In fact, you are probably the last person she'll listen to when you ask her to stop inviting her boyfriend to stay overnight—your history together will make her defensive or angry and cause her to misinterpret your intention. In addition, it's possible that the mom is complicit in the neglect or verbal abuse. She may have rationalized the behavior because she's desperate to keep the boyfriend or she's in denial about what's going on.

Finally, keep in mind that the courts recognize a wide variety of situations and behaviors that may be damaging to a child in these cases. Don't assume that your wife is immune from the court's intervention because there's no physical danger to the kids from the boyfriend. Intimidation and threats, sexual promiscuity, abuse of drugs and alcohol when the kids are present, and other behaviors all can be considered by the court as actionable. Supervision, counseling, and removal of a child from the home are possible consequences.

Remarriage: New Spouse, Old Problems

Most divorced dads aren't prepared for the issues that arise when they remarry. Women tend to be savvier than men about the implications of starting a second family; men tend to be blindsided by the responses of their second wives to their first ones.

Here's an example of one of the biggest problems that divorced dads face when they remarry. Our client, Cliff, called our office sobbing only days after his second wife gave birth to his new daughter. His divorce had settled, both he and his ex were happy with the settlement, and he was being a good divorced dad and fully present in his time with his kids from the first marriage. Now, with a new baby with a wife he loved, Cliff should have been ecstatic. Instead, he was tremendously upset. It turned out that his new wife had just given him an ultimatum: stop seeing your ex, stop seeing your kids on your visitation days, and stop paying them child support or this marriage is over.

Admittedly this was an extreme demand. But what's not unusual is a second wife placing restrictions on the amount of time and money a man can spend on his first family. It often becomes a control issue: the second wife feels threatened by the first one, even when there's no reason to feel this way. But she sees how much he loves his kids, how much time he's spending with them, and how often he sees or speaks with his former spouse. When this second wife has a baby, she naturally wants and needs more of her husband's time, and money often becomes a greater concern (because she's not working or because of the expenses associated with having a new child). She sees him paying a significant amount of money in support and leaving the house for visitation when she needs him to help her at home, and she tries to control the situation.

If you're in this type of situation, do the following:

- Fulfill your legal and parental obligations. Don't do what Cliff did: he stopped seeing his children and stopped paying child support, facing jail time as a result. Instead, recognize that you have responsibilities to both families, and do what you have to do to fulfill them both. If you have a spouse who insists you choose, as Cliff's second wife did, you and she need to talk to a therapist and a good divorce attorney—the former to help you work through issues of anger, jealousy, and control and the latter to explain the legal implications of not paying child support.

- Communicate what your rights and obligations are to your new wife (preferably before you remarry). One of the first things you should do is share with her the terms of your divorce settlement. Clarify what you need to do to be a good divorced dad in terms of visitation, communication with your ex, and so on. Explain your support payments and how they work. This knowledge can go a long way to avoiding misunderstandings about why you're spending so much time over at your ex-wife's house or why you're paying so much money to them.

- Talk about and plan for a second set of kids. Many times, the second wives of divorced dads don't start having control issues until they have a child. New moms are under a great deal of stress in any situation, but when they need dad around to help change diapers and run errands and he says he has to go over to his ex-wife's house to see the other set of kids, she blows her top. Don't let it reach this point. Talk in advance about the potential conflicts that will arise when you start a new family, and create a plan to deal with these conflicts. Arrange for a friend or relative to keep your wife company when you fulfill your obligations to your children from the first marriage. Discuss what your options are when your wife needs you at home because the baby is being cranky and it's your visitation time with your other children.

In addition, remarriage often means that kids from one marriage will mix with kids from another marriage. For divorced dads who don't have custody, the big issue is what happens when your kids mix with your ex's new husband's kids. If, for instance, your ex marries a guy who has kids and she brings her children into the household, she naturally wants everything to go smoothly. If fighting and bullying are taking place among the children, she may choose to ignore it. She may worry that the tension between the children will create tension between herself and her new husband; they may have already had arguments about "his kids" versus "her kids," and she is loathe to bring up the subject again.

Good divorced dads pay attention to these situations. By "pay attention," I mean that you should watch and listen closely. When you are over at your ex's residence, do the children from both marriages play together? Do you notice if one kid often bullies another one or the group picks on one child? Does it seem as if either parent's kids are favored in various ways—for example, that they have much nicer clothes, bigger rooms, better toys? Or are they favored in terms of not being punished for the same offenses the other children are punished for?

Just as important, pay strict attention to what your kids tell you about their stepsiblings. They may be direct about their feelings: "I hate my stepbrother!" They may also be subtle. Fearful of incurring the wrath of their stepdad or disappointing their mom, they may be reluctant to tell you that they're being bullied or hit by a stepsibling. Watch for signs that something is going on. Perhaps they constantly mention a stepbrother and something he said or did in a way that puzzles you; you're not sure what they're trying to communicate. Maybe they never mention a particular stepsibling, as if they're fearful of even uttering his name. It's up to you to pay attention to any sign of a problem and then intervene with their mom if you think you need to become involved.

Be especially vigilant if your ex remarries someone whose children are older than your own and if they're the same sex as your kids. This sets up classic bullying scenarios. I had one client whose wife remarried and her new husband had custody of two girls who were older than my client's daughter. At first, my client assumed his child was going to be in a comfortable situation: the father made a lot of money and could provide her with a nice home in a great neighborhood. In addition, the stepfather seemed like a good person. He knew his ex was overjoyed to marry someone with money—they'd been struggling since he was laid off from his job. For this reason, my client was unaware for months that the new husband's daughters were verbally abusing his daughter constantly. At one point, they took her pet cat and put it in the oven, threatening to cook it. His daughter, who was very young, never said anything about any of this to our client because the mother told her, "They're just teasing you," and "Don't be a tattletale." Months of this verbal torture went on before my client figured out what was happening, and only through legal intervention were we able to put a stop to it.

This example brings up yet another issue that comes with remarriage. As you struggle to meet your support payments, you discover that your ex is marrying someone who makes three times as much as you do. Logically you figure that you won't have to pay as much in support now that your children's mom is living an affluent lifestyle. Perhaps she is able to quit her job because of her newly found wealth. Perhaps she's driving a late-model luxury car while you're driving a beater. You can see that your children are being well provided for. Can you reduce your support?

Probably not. As unfair as it may seem, the courts are not inclined to change the support amount if the only factor that has changed since the settlement is that your ex has married a wealthy man. Similarly, if you marry a wealthy woman, they probably won't give in to a request from your ex that you pay more.

There are, however, exceptions to this general rule. If your support payment is based on a low yearly income—let's say twenty thousand dollars annually—and you marry into wealth, the courts will probably be more inclined to grant a request for increased support. Their rationale would be that you weren't providing your kids with a reasonable amount of support and that they're entitled to that reasonable amount if you can afford it. Again, generally, they are less inclined to grant reductions in support in these remarriage situations where your ex has married a wealthy person. However, in some states (Illinois is one of them) the courts may be inclined to grant a reduction or what is legally termed a "deviation"—from 20 percent of your net income to 10 percent for one child, for instance—if you can prove that extenuating circumstances now exist that justify a reduction. For instance, say that you are now supporting an aging parent, or you have a child with special needs from your new marriage who is costing you a lot of money. As long as the mom has significant resources to provide for the kids, the court may grant this deviation.

Being a good divorced dad means providing financial support for your children if you are able to do so. At the same time, if you're under tremendous financial stress and it's obvious that the kids' mom has acquired significant wealth through remarriage, you have every right to talk to your lawyer about the situation and petition the court for a deviation.

There's one other remarriage financial issue you should be aware of. Let's say your ex is a vengeful person or has emotional problems. Let's further assume that she remarries someone who has a great deal of money. In these instances, she may choose to use her newly found wealth to manipulate the legal system to your disadvantage. I had a client who was just scraping by, and his wife remarried a wealthy man after he divorced her. My client was handsome and charming, but he was not good at holding a job for long. He was the one who ended the marriage, and his ex never forgave him. When she remarried, she chose to use some of her new wealth to aggravate him because he occasionally missed a support payment. These payments were only one hundred dollars, and she had access to millions to provide for their child, but as she told my client, her goal was to have him thrown in jail for nonsupport. Fortunately, the judge in the case recognized what she was trying to do and refused to jail him.

If your children's mother is vengeful in this way, you need to do everything possible to make your support payments and stay out of jail. A good lawyer should be able to make a convincing case that your ex is acting out of vengeance rather than in the best interest of the child. Recognize, too, that if your child has a vengeful mother, he especially needs you to stay out of jail and stay in his life. Talk to your lawyer about what you need to do to avoid being victimized by her legal shenanigans. Justice should not be a luxury only the rich can afford. Two recommendations are to avoid doing anything that triggers this vengeful impulse, especially after she marries a wealthy man, and adhere to the letter of the requirements of your settlement so you don't give her grounds to go after you.

As we'll see in the next chapter, this is only one of many financial issues that divorced dads need to understand and confront, not just for their own sake but for the sake of their kids.

CHAPTER 5

Money Issues

How to Manage Changing and Challenging Financial Situations

It should go without saying that men want to provide for their children; the desire to provide is hard-wired into us. Divorce doesn't diminish this impulse, but it does create situations that can prevent dads from providing for their kids consistently.

Some fathers struggle with anxiety and depression after a divorce, and they may be so down that they lose their jobs as well as the income needed to pay support. Some respond to a mom who denies them rightful visitation by withholding support payments until she restores visitation privileges. Some men reduce or stop their support payments when their exes remarry wealthy men who provide a much better financial life for the kids than they ever could.

These and other actions related to money have serious negative repercussions from a legal standpoint. Good divorced dads learn how to deal with these situations with the best interest of their children as their guide rather than their anger or shame.

The financial challenges you're going to face depend on three key factors. Let's examine these factors and the best ways to respond to them.

Three Key Money Matters

When someone like actor Bruce Willis or any wealthy person gets divorced, his support issues are going to be different from those of an out-of-work dad who dropped out of high school. Similarly, if you fathered a child out of wedlock and never had a DNA test, you may face legal challenges that are different from someone who had a child within the framework of a marriage. The point is that your ability to provide support and feel good about yourself as a father depends to a certain extent on your situation.

Let's say you had a child out of wedlock, an increasingly common occurrence for many reasons (over half of the children born in Cook County in Illinois, for example, are born out of wedlock). Though you face many of the same parenting challenges as someone who was married and divorced, you also may encounter a different type of financial issue. I realize that the next few paragraphs may not be directly relevant to you if you didn't father a child out of wedlock, but there's a lesson here for all dads: don't let the legal system discourage you from doing everything possible to protect your relationship with your child.

Typically what happens is that you and your partner are living together and have a child. For a while, things go great. But then the relationship breaks up, and you move out. Perhaps the two of you informally agree that you'll provide a certain amount of support in exchange for which you get to see the child whenever you want. On the surface, this sounds like a far better deal than you can get if you go through the legal system: you avoid all the legal costs and you are able to see your child more often than a formal visitation agreement might allow. The problem is that when conflict occurs, and a conflict between separated parents is almost inevitable, your former partner as the custodial parent has all the power.

In many instances, this conflict involves money. Your child's mom demands more financial assistance, and you don't think what she's asking for is justified or you simply lack the money to pay it. She responds by saying that until you agree to her terms, you can't see your child. Without the protection of a paternity order and court-approved support and visitation terms, you don't have a legal leg to stand on.

Proving paternity this late in the game can take time and money, as can going to court and hammering out a custody agreement, child support payments, and so on. Many men are so intimidated by this process that they just give up—they stop supporting and seeing their kids. Just as troubling, some men decide they will go through the legal process, but in the interim, they don't see their kids for months and their mom uses this time to alienate the kids from their dad (often because she's furious at him for not agreeing to her terms or forcing her to go through the legal process, or both).

Therefore, I urge you to establish paternity on the birth of your child and secure a legally blessed agreement for custody, support, and visitation as soon as the relationship stops working. The longer you delay, the more problematic your situation will become. In fact, consider a situation that is not uncommon and can be extremely expensive. You and your partner have a child, and shortly after the birth, you break up. A few years pass, and though you give some money to the child's mom for support, she doesn't ask you for much because her well-off parents are helping out. Then, because of some poor investments, her parents can no longer provide her with the money, so she goes to court and you're ordered to take a DNA test. Once it's determined that you are the father of the child, the court orders you to start making regular support payments; even more surprising, you're required to pay thousands of dollars in support arrearages (accumulated money owed for support since your child was born) you can't afford.

Many men become so upset or discouraged in this situation— or they find that they lack the money to make the payments the court orders—that they sever their relationship with their child. This is yet another reason that you should establish paternity and hire an attorney as soon as you realize that the prospects that the relationship will continue are poor. In fact, if you decide to have a child with your partner out of wedlock, you should see a lawyer while the relationship is going well and establish a legal contingency plan for custody, support, or visitation in the event that the relationship doesn't work out. This contingency plan isn't just to protect you, but to ensure that your child will receive the financial support he or she is entitled to, as well as the regular emotional contact he or she needs from you.

The second situational factor is about your custody arrangement. Ideally you and your ex will agree on joint custody, since this should give you more participation in all the financial decisions that affect your child: whether to send her to private school, spend the money on music lessons, and so on. When you have joint custody and have a disagreement about how money is to be spent, you will likely go through court-ordered mediation; if that doesn't work, you go to court. In the majority of cases, however, men automatically accept noncustodial-parent status and generally must pay a certain amount of child support: 20 percent of their net income for one child and incrementally more for each additional child is a common percentage in many states. The premise of support payments is that the custodial parent is inherently responsible for more child-related expenses than the noncustodial parent (providing a residence, clothing, and so forth), so you are likely to be ordered to contribute your statutory share.

I urge dads who are looking to have joint custody to seek that initial determination first and then collaborate with the child's mom to determine a fair support payment.

The third factor is your financial net worth and income. As a general rule, the more money you have, the more likely that support payments and other financial issues will interfere with your ability to be a good dad. This may seem counterintuitive, but generally wealthy individuals tend to be more materialistic than those who have less, or, to put it another way, there's more to fight over. Money becomes a symbol and therefore a hotly contested issue both during the divorce and afterward. Both moms and dads, as well as their attorneys, can lose sight of how their financial battles are affecting the children. As a result, some moms ask for unreasonable amounts of money for support to punish dads; they also make arguments for additional payments involving everything from clothes to cars that are designed to irritate their exes (rather than because their children really need these things). In turn, some dads may battle against reasonable requests for support because they are angry. They may also force an overly materialistic mom and the kids to move to a smaller residence not because they can't afford the larger one but because they know that their ex-wife will hate the fall in status and blow to her ego.

If you happen to be in the fortunate position of being in this high-income category, recognize that as angry as you may be and as much as your ex may deserve your ire, using support as a weapon against her will likely backfire. Ask your lawyer what's fair in terms of support for your children and their other financial needs. Even if you're square in the middle-income category, focus on doing the right thing for your children rather than on exacting a pound of flesh. When you use support payments vengefully, you end up hurting yourself and your children more than your ex.

Keep in mind the following quotation: "One hundred years from now, it will not matter what my bank account was, the sort of house I lived in, or the kind of car I drove . . . but the world may be different because I was important in the life of a child."[1]

Mistakes and Misconceptions

While mistakes and misconceptions about divorce abound, the ones about money are more numerous and potentially more devastating to dads than in any other category. That's because men often measure themselves by the money they make and their ability to provide for their families. When they fall victim to mistakes and misconceptions, they often diminish both their financial worth and their self-worth.

Let's examine the most common errors divorced dads make, their impact on the children, and how to prevent these missteps.

Failing to Document Cash Payments

Some divorced dads arrange to provide their ex with cash for whatever the children need or just give her money whenever she asks for it. They feel that they and their wife are two civilized people and that rather than involve the courts in how they support their family, they'll deal with it on their own. Or perhaps they are paying court-ordered support by cash, or they pay part with checks but provide additional cash payments when their ex requests it.

The problem, of course, is that there is no record of these cash payments. At some point in the future, the ex-wife may petition the court for money she says the dad owes her. But the dad lacks a record of his payments and so may be socked with a huge arrearage. Many dads doubt that this will ever happen to them, since they claim they have a good, trusting relationship with the children's mom. But all sorts of events can drive a wedge between ex-spouses, and at that point, the mom may feel justified in lying to the court in order to extract more money.

For this reason, keep a record of every dollar you give to your ex for support. Save money order receipts, canceled checks, and the like. If you don't have evidence of your payments and your ex pulls some stunt like the one just suggested, you'll feel devastated: you trusted her, and she took advantage of you. You may not have the money to pay the arrearage. You may be placed in a precarious financial position because of this mistake. In either case, your self-esteem will suffer. You may take it out in verbal and legal battles with your ex, or you may just feel lousy about yourself. In both instances, your kids will suffer. The fights may cause your spouse to deny you visitation, a possibly illegal but often effective tactic, or may speak negatively to your children about you, causing a rift in your relationship with them.

Substituting Gifts for Support Payments

Instead of paying court-ordered support, some dads think they can provide an equivalent amount of merchandise. They buy groceries or new bikes or clothes, and perhaps the ex is fine with this—for a while. However, if you do this, as with paying in cash, you run the risk that if and when your ex needs money, she'll go to court and you'll be assessed an arrearage for all the support payments you "missed." Most courts never credit these gifts toward support, and you will likely pay double. Such an arrearage can devastate dads and cause them to become depressed and uncommunicative or even incarcerated for contempt.

Creating Informal Agreements with an Ex If You Lose Your Job or Suffer a Financial Setback

You're suddenly downsized out of a job, or your investments or your business suffers a setback. You've been making your regular court-ordered support payments for weeks, months, even years, and you go to your ex and explain the situation and ask her if she will let you slide until your financial fortunes improve. You may even agree to try and pay as much as you can during this period, and she tells you this is fine; they'll make do until you get another job.

Unfortunately, mom's largesse may end if she experiences her own financial difficulties. She can go to court and demand you pay the arrearage, which consists of all missed or partial payments. Your informal agreement is worthless in court. Many men, however, aren't thinking clearly about these issues when they lose their job or suffer some other financial setback. Worried about money, the last thing they want to do is see their lawyer and incur legal fees. Thus, the informal agreement seems like a better alternative.

Assuming That You Won't Have to Pay More Than the State-Recommended Support Percentage of Income

When Bill and Tina were divorcing, Bill decided he didn't need an attorney since the only real financial issue involved his support payment to Tina for their four-year-old daughter. Bill knew what the state-mandated guideline percentage for support was, and he was fine with it. What he wasn't fine with was that the judge ordered him to pay support 10 percent above the statutory guideline. It turns out that his wife's attorney had made the case that their daughter had special needs that required additional money now and in the foreseeable future. His wife claimed that their child was a musical prodigy and that she would need money for private lessons, new violins, and other related expenses. In fact, their child was moderately talented and had taken lessons but showed no great aptitude for or interest in music. Nonetheless, Tina's attorney had made a convincing argument, and the court granted her request for a payment 10 percent above the guideline. In most states, this guideline is recommended, not inviolate.

Similarly, many fathers don't realize that they can petition for and receive a below-statutory-guideline support order. I'm not suggesting that this is easy to obtain. But if you legitimately can't afford the payment mandated by the statutory guideline, you're entitled to request a lesser amount. Dads who have a legitimate special needs child from another marriage, for instance, can be granted a lesser support payment for another child from their current divorce.

Believing That Your Financial Obligations to Your Child Begin and End with Support

This is an extraordinarily common misconception. Dads figure that 20 percent of their net income should always cover everything and that if mom (as the custodial parent) wants to buy a fancy dress for their daughter or enroll their son in swimming classes, that's her business—and her expense. In fact, many expenses arise that are unanticipated when support is ordered by the court. Child care may be necessary if the mom has to go back to work after the divorce. Summer camp is another common expense.

Some dads also mistakenly believe that their financial obligation to their child always ends when he or she reaches the age of eighteen. In fact, dads can be required to contribute significantly to college expenses—expenses that can top 20 percent of their net income for one child.

Good divorced dads don't protest against a fair expenditure of money. Don't deny your child braces for his teeth or a great camp experience with her friends if you can afford it. Don't allow your anger at their mom to cloud your strategic thinking. It is possible that she is being vindictive when she demands payments for certain things, but you need to analyze the value of any given request to your child. If it's something that's important to your kid and you can afford it, don't get enmeshed in a battle because your ex is baiting you into an argument. But if there's a pattern of requested expenditures that strikes you as unreasonable and purely vindictive, that's the time to contact your lawyer and challenge them. This is especially true if there's a limited amount of money available to spend on your child and he's going without and your ex is badgering you for things that are irrelevant to his health and happiness but are really earmarked for herself.

Believing That the Judge Will Ensure That the Support Agreement Is Fair

Many judges are unbiased and certainly intend for these agreements to be fair, but in reality, they often lack the time to study agreements carefully and spot all the unfair aspects. In many states, judges are responsible only for making sure the support agreement is not "unconscionable." In Illinois, for example, a settled divorce proceeding ends in a "prove-up" in which grounds for the divorce and the terms of it are recited before the judge. Typically prove-ups last only ten minutes and often are perfunctory. Unless a judge studies what can be a twenty-page complex document outlining the support and property provisions for a much longer period of time, he or she is not likely to spot everything that is unfair.

For this reason, don't allow your spouse's attorney to prepare the settlement agreement without benefit of your own attorney's participating in the process. You may trust your soon-to-be-ex-wife, but her attorney may have convinced her to include certain provisions that may turn out to be onerous. Or if you are in an emotionally traumatized state during the divorce, you may agree to an excessive payment or other terms that you'll resent later. What you want to avoid is anything in the agreement that will cause conflict between you and your ex because this conflict can result in pitched legal battles down the line that dissipate assets that should be there for your children in the future.

A House Divided: A Child-Centered Split of Marital Assets

When a marriage ends and parents start discussing who gets what, the house they've lived in often takes on meaning far beyond its market value. A divorcing couple can fight a pitched battle over the house that is destructive to them and their children. Typically the issue is whether the custodial parent and the child can continue to live in the house after the marriage ends.

Good divorced dads don't force mom and the kids to leave the house when it's unnecessary. Realistically, however, many men can't stand the thought of their ex continuing to live in a residence they bought and paid for; even worse, they can't tolerate the thought that their ex may remarry and the new guy, maybe even someone who destroyed their marriage, will live in "their" house. This is true even when moms contributed money to the purchase of a residence. Psychologically, men usually take great pride in family and home ownership and resent that someone who contributed nothing (the mom's new husband) lives there.

As irksome as this idea is, think about your children and what's meaningful for them. Is it better to uproot your kids—especially if they are young and reeling from the divorce—and cause them to live somewhere unfamiliar when you don't have to? Ideally you'll look for a way to allow the children to stay in familiar surroundings. To help you find that way, here are three steps you should take.

Consider Making a Swap Between Your Retirement Plan and the House

When a client comes to me and says that the equity in his marital retirement fund is approximately the same as his equity in the marital home, I usually suggest his wife waive her interest in his retirement plan and he transfer to his ex his interest in the house. Most women will agree to this swap not only because it allows them and the children to remain there but also because they have a strong emotional attachment to the home. And you're not only doing the right thing by your children, but probably helping improve your own financial future. A retirement plan generally is creditor proof—that is, most creditors can't seize it no matter how your financial situation might deteriorate. But a house is often vulnerable to seizure by creditors in most instances if the mortgage isn't paid or repairs become so costly that it's better to get rid of it.

Refrain from Joint Ownership of the House After the Divorce

You may be tempted to pursue this option as a provision in the marital settlement agreement, especially if you have a strong emotional attachment to the house or you believe it's a great investment that will pay off in the future. You talk with your ex and decide that you'll share equally in the house's upkeep and split the profits equally when the last child leaves home and you're ready to sell.

More often than not, though, this arrangement leads to major battles with your former spouse. Some of the battles involve whether repairs are necessary—you're more likely to say no because you don't live there. Other arguments revolve around additions, renovations, and even decorating. Refinancing is another area of potential dispute. The fact is that the house becomes a flashpoint for arguments, activating any dormant tension between you and your ex. It also will become a growing irritant in your life. You may say to yourself, "I no longer live there and enjoy the place, but I'm still paying through the nose for it." And unless you're affluent, it's difficult to maintain two residences, so you may have to rent for years instead of own your place.

Remember that your kids will benefit if you can establish a civil relationship with their mom, and houses often prevent that relationship from being civil. If you can't work out a deal in which your ex as the custodial parent owns the house, you may need to sell it. Be aware, though, that if you sell, you and your ex might not split the proceeds equally. If you can't agree on a fair percentage split, the judge will intervene and determine what's fair. Many times judges favor the custodial parent and provide her with a larger percentage of the sale's proceeds than the noncustodial parent.

Put Extra Assets in an Irrevocable Trust for Kids

Responsible fathers recognize that they can't always leave providing for the kids up to the moms, especially if they know those moms aren't particular good with saving money. If there is extra money because of the divorce—if your agreement calls for you to sell houses, cars, artwork, and so on—then consider investing what you can afford in an irrevocable trust for the benefit of your children. As the term implies, this trust is likely permanent and protected. The money you put in it should always be there for your children, and you can't remove it from the trust later if you become angry at your children or for any other reason. Similarly, this trust should prevent both you and your kids' creditors from seizing it as an asset. By setting up this trust, you're ensuring that the money will be there when your kids need it—for emergencies, to help pay for college, and so on. You should consider putting these assets in a trust as soon after the divorce as possible. Hard experience shows that your share of the marital assets tends to be dissipated over time, in part because living apart (from the kids' mom) is usually more expensive than living together.

When Financial Circumstances Change

You may be diligent about providing your children with financial support for months, even years after the divorce. You never miss a support payment. You find a way to pay for whatever is important in their lives above and beyond support. You avoid pitched battles with your ex over money. You're doing everything right. And then something changes.

One possible financial change is an increase in wealth. You may inherit a significant sum of money or receive a major gift (your elderly parents gift you a significant sum of money or their summer home, for instance). Or your ex may be the beneficiary of similar events. In either case, be aware that many states view gifts as income for setting child support. Therefore, a significant gift may have an impact on your support payments. You need to consult with your lawyer relative to the law in your state, but regardless of what that law is, judges have a great deal of discretion to set support amounts and secure assets in the best interests of children. Therefore, they will likely pay attention to whom is receiving gifts and it may influence their decisions about support.

Bill was furious when his ex divorced him because she was seeing another man. So when Bill's attorney told him he could not expect to get a reduction in support for his two young children after the divorce went through based on his income, Bill conspired with his boss (also a divorced dad) to fire him. "No income, no support," or so Bill reasoned. He figured he could get by on his savings for a while, and besides, he had a significant amount of money invested in real estate. Because this investment provided no current income—though the capital appreciation was good and growing—Bill figured it wouldn't have an impact on his support payment. In fact, the judge ordered support based on imputed income (that is, your estimated income in the absence of definitive records such as tax returns and paychecks) from Bill's real estate investments and income he would have been receiving if still employed because he voluntarily relinquished his employment.

I've seen instances where judges ordered support payments even though dads had no income for years. In these instances, a sizable gift existed, the dad had major investments, or he had substantial savings from previous well-paying jobs. I've also seen judges order trusts to be set up for children and transfer a portion of a dad's assets into the trust that the dad can't touch until the children are grown, usually to make sure child support is paid. Judges may take an action like this if an individual has a history of failing to make regular support payments, for instance.

Your financial situation can also deteriorate: you might lose your job or suffer some other financial setback, an experience that can be devastating to a man's psyche and drive a wedge between him and his kids. Lowered financial worth sometimes equates to lowered self-esteem. Some dads are so embarrassed that they don't have the income to meet their child support payments that they cut off contact with their families or become so depressed that it changes how they relate to their children.

If you find yourself in this situation, you need to do two things. First, inform your lawyer about your financial situation. He or she can petition the court for a reduction in support payments or explore other alternatives until you get back on your feet. Second, seek emotional help if you need it. Even if you can't afford therapy, there may be a men's support group or other type of support in your area that provides free or low-cost assistance.

The Deadbeat Dad Myth

The term *deadbeat dad* is widely recognized as a way to describe fathers who fail to pay child support. As we'll see in a bit, this term can devastate men who care deeply about supporting their kids but are prohibited from doing so by unforeseen circumstances. These men aren't "deadbeat"; they're dead broke. Certainly fathers exist who refuse to support their children out of anger at the mom, selfishness, or cheapness, but I also want to make it clear that they have their counterpart in "deadbeat moms."

I'm not referring here to mothers who are noncustodial parents and refuse to pay support to dads (though these moms exist). Instead, I'm talking about mothers who take the support money they receive and spend it on themselves rather than on their children. If you have a joint custody agreement, a process is in place for you and your ex to consult and decide about all major expenditures. If the mom has custody, however, she is generally under no obligation to account for how she spends the money you give her, at least in most states. The courts assume that her expenditures will benefit the child, either directly or indirectly, even if they don't.

But let's say you notice that your ex, who you know is strapped for money, shows up wearing a new designer outfit every other month or has managed to purchase a luxury car, and you also become aware that your children's shoes are worn out and that they aren't allowed to go on school trips or participate in extra-curricular activities that require payment. Even under these circumstances, you have relatively little legal recourse. Unless the behavior is outrageous—the kids are going hungry or are living in a hovel while she is driving a fancy new car and wearing new diamonds—courts are reluctant to become involved.

In some states, you can ask the court to allow you to make direct payments for certain necessities for your kids rather than have the money pass through the mom. You may also request judicial supervision of the mom to ensure that someone in authority is monitoring how she spends the money you give her. The courts in most states, however, tend to be reluctant to grant either of these options. Instead, they prefer that dads file for sole custody if they have evidence that the mom is not providing for the children properly. If you do have this evidence, consult with your attorney and consider whether this is a strategy worth pursuing.

Now let's turn to deadbeat dads. According to the largest federally funded study (a U.S. Government Accountability Office survey) of divorced dads ever conducted, unemployment rather than willful neglect was the main reason for failure to pay child support.[2] In a survey of custodial mothers who were owed support, it found that two-thirds of the fathers weren't paying because they were indigent.

If you're characterized by society as a deadbeat dad, therefore, the odds are that you're not the lowlife that the term suggests but probably have just fallen on hard times. The odds are that you want to support your child but lack the money to do so. It's also possible that you have the money but your ex is holding your kids hostage and won't let you see them unless you pay more in support. According to the Children's Rights Council, custodial parents interfere with noncustodial parents' access to 5 million kids annually. If your ex prevents you from seeing your kids, you may feel that your only recourse is not to send any support until you're allowed to see them again.

Although this response is a mistake, this figure of 5 million children suggests why many dads who have money may fall into the deadbeat category: they want to see their children, and they don't want to pay extortion in order to do so. If you want to be a good divorced dad, don't let the situation reach this point or take legal action as soon as it does.

Readjust Your Attitude

Financial problems destroy more marriages than love affairs by a long shot. There is a saying in family law circles: when the bills come in the door, love flies out the window. A lost job or other significant financial loss creates tremendous tension in the marriage. Not only do these financial setbacks catalyze arguments between mom and dad, they make the breadwinner (still usually the father) feel worthless. It may cause him to withdraw from his wife first and his kids next. If these financial issues are the cause of the divorce, he may feel responsible for letting his family down and think that his children aren't interested in seeing him.

This thinking is not only erroneous, but it causes further problems for your kids. It's not unusual for a couple to divorce and then months or even years later, one or both of them must declare bankruptcy. It is always more expensive to support two households rather than one, and if neither remarries, each is trying to get by on less. When the dad feels so despondent about how his financial difficulties caused the divorce, he may lack the drive necessary to get or hold a good job. In some situations, this results in home foreclosures and other negative events, all of which hurt the children.

What I urge dads to do in these situations is to use the divorce as an opportunity to get their financial house in order. Make a concerted effort to be fiscally stable: don't spend more than you can afford on luxuries, and don't pile up credit card debt. View the divorce as an opportunity for a fresh start in both your personal and your professional life. If you need to both work and go back to school to improve your chances of getting a better-paying job, do it. Be serious about your career. Having a good, well-paying job will go a long way to helping you not only support your children but improve your self-image, both crucial to being a good divorced dad.

CHAPTER 6

When There's a New Man in Your Children's Life

How to Avoid Being Replaced

The good news is that if you're an emotionally involved, physically present father, you can't be replaced. It doesn't matter if your ex remarries someone, even if that person has more money than you do and treats your children to all sorts of trips and gifts you can't afford. Blood is thicker than water, money, or any other connective medium.

Let me tell you a story that makes this point. Tanya was a seventeen year old who had not seen her father since she was a three years old. He had been incarcerated since that time, and Tanya's mother never had anything good to say about him. She had remarried years ago, and Tanya had a solid relationship with her stepfather. Nonetheless, when Tanya heard that her father was going to be in court for a hearing in the city where she was living, she decided she wanted to attend just to see him. She didn't plan to say anything or even acknowledge him, but when he was led into the courtroom handcuffed, with a cop on either side of him, she couldn't help herself. She ran up to him, shouting, "Daddy, Daddy," and embraced him.

Tanya's father was neither emotionally involved nor physically present, but the bond between daughter and divorced dad remained powerful. I'm not suggesting that you should take that bond for granted. If you're an absent father, your kids may not respond as Tanya did and you might never be able to repair the damage your absence causes. But I relate this story to remind you that you're difficult to replace.

If you're like many other divorced dads, you need reminding. That's because when your children's mom brings a new man into their lives, you may well feel as if you have been pushed out of the picture. But even if that is your ex-wife's intent, it won't work— unless you allow it to happen.

To make sure that you take advantage of the bond you have with your children and remain a continuous presence in their lives, let's start by categorizing the different men who may assume father figure roles in your kids' lives.

From Stepfathers to Psychological Dads

Understanding the different men moms bring into children's lives is important for a number of reasons. First, it helps you determine if someone is a positive or negative (or neutral) influence on your kids. Second, this knowledge can diminish your fears when you know how each type is likely to relate to your children and the roles they often assume. Third, it puts your legal rights into perspective and helps you know when and what you can do if you feel you're being pushed aside.

Here are five types of men (some overlap exists between types and some people are more than one type):

- *The psychological father.* These men are not stepfathers (they are not married to your ex, but they are either living in the same residence or are a frequent presence), but they are invested in taking care of the kids. Even though they aren't the biological dads, they establish good relationships with your children, and your kids view them as authority figures who take on responsibilities.

- *The nonpsychological, coparent alienator.* These guys, who may be stepfathers or boyfriends, not only don't take on a parental role but they conspire with your ex to create a wedge between you and your children. Their attitude has a negative influence on your relationship with your kids.

- *The good stepfather.* He becomes a psychological parent, invested emotionally in parenting responsibilities. In some instances, he becomes a coparent not only to your ex but to you—he works with you to raise the kids the right way and is supportive of you. Although it's unrealistic to expect that this type would side with you and against your ex on any significant issue, you may come to trust and rely on him when it comes to your kids.

- *The bad stepfather.* This individual might be a parental alienator. At worst, he could also be verbally, physically, or sexually abusive to your children. Because he's around them all the time, he can do a lot of damage. This is the man you need to watch out for and take legal action, if necessary, to prevent him from doing harm.

- *Adoptive father.* This father legally takes over your role as dad. If you break contact with your ex and kids—in order to avoid child support payments or for other reasons—this man likely goes through the legal process of adopting your kids. You have no rights as a father once this legal process is completed. In other instances, adoption may take place because you're convicted of a crime or judged to be an unfit dad for other reasons. Remember, though, that the courts are strongly biased in favor of biological parents, so it takes an egregious act for adoption to take place (or for some reason, you voluntarily give up all rights).

- *The boyfriend.* This man is there not for your children but for your ex. He may neglect the children or even abuse them. Or he may be indifferent toward them. It's possible that boyfriends may be kind and establish a relationship with your kids, but the danger, especially for smaller children, is that they form a relationship with your kids and then disappear from their lives.

Recognizing these distinctions is crucial, since it will help you determine the actions to take that are in the best interest of your children. For instance, some dads observe a series of rotating, live-in boyfriends who bond with their children and then depart, traumatizing their kids. Good divorced dads don't tolerate this, even though they may be secretly glad that the boyfriend their son or daughter talked so much about is out of the picture. If this happens to you, you need to help your ex act more responsibly and protect your children through discussion with your ex, mediation, or legal action. Mediation is an especially useful forum for this type of discussion, since many dads aren't comfortable talking with their ex about her choice of boyfriends. An unbiased mediator, however, is in a position to raise this issue and a mom's awareness of how it's affecting the kids. Talk to your lawyer about the best approach for your particular circumstances.

At the other end of the spectrum, your ex may remarry a man who becomes a true psychological parent to your kids. Remember, though, that he has no legal rights as a father. Your biological connection to your children plus your legal rights will ensure that you'll always come first in their hearts and minds, assuming you are a physically and emotionally present parent. In fact, some divorced dads come to rely on stepdads to communicate with their exes on certain touchy issues; the stepfathers aren't emotionally invested in the issues and can sometimes get messages across in ways that dads can't.

The new man in your ex's and children's lives may be a positive rather than a negative influence. Before feeling resentful, depressed, or angry because of the mere existence of this man, get to know what kind of person he is in terms of his relationship with your ex and with your children. Don't jump to conclusions; get to know him through personal interactions as well as through what your ex and your kids say about him. In this way, you're less likely to experience the sense that you're being replaced.

Typical Reactions and Scenarios

Without taking the time and making the effort to know what your ex's new man is like, you're going to react badly the first time you drop your child off at mom's house and see him hug this guy or when your child talks nonstop about how his stepfather took him to the zoo, bought him ice cream, has this cool car, and so on. It may be, too, that your ex or this man is manipulating situations to make you feel excluded and alienated from your children.

You need to be aware of the typical divorced dad reaction when your ex brings a guy into her house and productive and unproductive ways to act in these situations. Most divorced dads respond to their ex's getting remarried by feeling threatened, angry, vulnerable, and emasculated. This is perfectly understandable, even if they initiated the divorce and no longer have strong feelings for their exes. All it takes is for their child's mom to brag that her new husband makes a lot more money, is kinder and more generous than you ever were, is more of a *real* man, and dads experience all the previous negative feelings. These emotions are exacerbated when their children express admiration for their stepdad and call him "Dad," or say or do anything that makes a divorced dad feel as if he's coming in second. Good divorced dads find this situation very painful.

Joe was married to Dena for twelve years. They had twin girls who were five years old at the time of the divorce, an amicable one. Both agreed that they would try to remain friends and make all the important decisions together; joint custody was something they both embraced right away. Two years later, Dena met Jason and a year after that married him. Although Joe thought Jason seemed like a good guy, he wasn't prepared for what it would be like dealing with his children's stepfather. It irritated him that Dena and the girls had moved into Jason's house, even though it made financial sense and allowed them to sell the old house and split the profits (between Joe and Dena). He also found it hurtful that when he picked up the girls, they talked nonstop about the places Jason had taken them and the funny things he said and did. Because Jason worked at home (he was a software consultant) and had flexible hours and Dena had an office job, he was the one who drove them places and did some of the shopping with them. Joe had just taken a new job that required a great deal of travel, and he often was unable to make all his visitation dates. Though Dena was good about letting him see the girls on nonvisitation days, he still felt as if the girls were transferring their love from him to Jason. He became so worried that he asked Dena to let the girls live with him over the summer when his schedule became less hectic. Dena refused, saying that he lived in a small apartment on the other side of town and it would be difficult for the girls to see their friends. Dena's refusal led to a huge argument between them, and it reached the point where Joe declared, "If I can't see my girls more, than I might as well not see them at all." Eventually he calmed down and worked out a mutually acceptable arrangement with Dena. But this story illustrates how painful it can be to see another man enter your children's orbit and how divorced dads can respond with anger, depression, and all the emotions in between.

Other dads try to just avoid stepfathers and boyfriends. For example, a dad learns that his son's stepfather is going to be attending his son's baseball game and declares, "If he's going, I'm not." Or when he and the stepfather are in the same room with the kids, he finds some reason to leave early. This may seem like a good plan, but over time, these dads spend less and less time with their children because they can't stand to be in the same room or house as the other guy. They make all sorts of excuses about why they can't be at this event or that one, but they are really responding to their pain due to the presence of another father figure in their child's life by avoiding him.

Perhaps the most common response is anger. In a bit, I'll talk about when this anger is justified and what you can do if you discover that there is a systematic attempt to exclude you from your kids' lives. Here, though, I want to alert you to some typical triggers for conflicts involving the mom's new guy that are fairly easily avoided:

- *The children call the stepfather or boyfriend "Dad."* This is generally a bad idea, especially for younger children, since it confuses them. In fact, one of the attorneys in our firm handled a case in which the mom instructed her children to call the stepdad "Papa" and call their dad by his first name, "Bill." This conflict went to court, and the judge ruled against the mom. In most instances, you can iron out this issue through informal discussion or mediation. Generally kids call stepparents by their first name.

- *Father's Day and other dad-centric celebrations.* You want your kids to be with you on this day and your ex thinks the kids should spend at least part of the day with their stepfather. In many men's minds, this seems to confer equal or preferential status on the stepfather, and they are willing to go to court to prevent this from happening. Ideally you have court-ordered visitation or parenting time to have your child with you on Father's Day, to have him celebrate your birthday with you, and so on. If not, it may be advisable to seek such legal safeguards. At the same time, remember that this may not be the issue over which you want to go to the mat, or to court, unless the situation is harmful to your kids or their relationship with you. As long as you are able to spend a significant amount of time with your child on a day that's special to both of you, that should usually be acceptable. It's better that stepfathers care enough about your child to want to be with him than to be indifferent, neglectful, or abusive.

- *School events*. You're surprised and upset to see the stepfather show up for parent-teacher conferences. Or after a school play or athletic event, your child spends most of her time with your ex and her new husband and their family and very little time with you. These situations are difficult for divorced dads to deal with; unfortunately, they are inevitable and ongoing. Whether through discussion or mediation, you need to work out a way to handle your own feelings as well as the logistics of attendance at school functions. Don't just simmer and stew over what you feel is inequitable or let the discomfort prevent you from attending at all. Focus on your child's relationship with you. This is about her, and she needs you to be at her conferences, plays, sports events, graduation, and other major events.

Recognize that these conflicts are inevitable, but that many of them can be resolved with relative ease if you deal with them rationally or with the assistance of competent, empathetic mediators, lawyers, and therapists. What's more difficult to resolve, however, is when your rights as a dad are being violated by your ex and her new spouse or boyfriend.

When You Are Being Subordinated or Ignored

It is difficult to be a good divorced dad if you are being shunted to the side. Typically this happens when your ex is angry at you. She knows how to hurt you, and what hurts most is being pushed out of your role as dad by your ex and her new husband or boyfriend. Whether it's a systematic effort or a random occurrence, it is something you should not tolerate. To determine if your ex is making an effort to diminish your role as dad and substitute another man in that role, answer the following questions:

- Do you find that this new man is taking over some or many of the responsibilities you used to have, like picking the kids up from school and going with them to doctor appointments?

- When you meet an adult who knows your children—a neighbor, a teacher, a coach—for the first time, does that person seem surprised that you're the dad because he or she assumed that the other man in their life is the father?

- Do you find that you're not being informed when your child has a medical problem, a school activity, or some other event where you're entitled to be present?

- Do your children tell you that your ex has told them not to pay attention to what you tell them to do because the stepfather is now their "real dad," or words to this effect?

- Are your children being raised in the religion of the stepfather rather than your own?

- If you have joint custody, are there decisions that you're supposed to make with your kids' mom that she is making unilaterally or with the stepfather?

- Is your ex finding ways to reduce the time you get to spend with your kids incrementally—having you spend an hour less on visitation days, for instance, or asking if she and her new husband can take the kids for a weekend when you're supposed to have them?

- Does this new man hang up on you when you call, interrupt when you try to talk to your kids, and find other ways to make your life miserable?

- When you come to pick up the kids, does your ex or the stepdad open the door an inch and peer out, as if a monster is seeking entry?

- Does your ex constantly compare you unfavorably to her husband, saying that he makes more money, that he's better with the kids, or something similar?

If you answered yes to one or more of these questions, then you may be vulnerable to your ex's strategy to get rid of you. As you can tell from the questions, sometimes the strategy involves a stepfather or boyfriend who is taking over responsibilities you used to have, and sometimes it's your ex trying to discourage you from spending time with the children. Sometimes her strategy is to employ psychological warfare: she makes it so unpleasant or difficult for you to spend time with the kids that you give up and tell yourself it's not worth it. Sometimes her strategy is more subtle, such as when she tells you that she's going to raise your children in a different religion from her own, which is the one her new spouse practices because, she says, religion is very important to him. It may not actually be very important to him, but she knows that telling you this will make you feel as if you're coming in second to his wishes and implies that what he wants is more important than what you want.

In these situations, there are a number of things you can do to protect your rights as a divorced dad and ensure that you remain as involved in your child's life as possible.

Talk to Your Lawyer

Begin by talking to your lawyer about your suspicions and determine the best course of action, legal or otherwise. Too often noncustodial dads assume that they're powerless in situations where it seems as if there's been no obvious violation of the divorce agreement. They figure the custodial parent has the power to diminish their parental role.

This may have been true in the past, but things are changing. For instance, the courts used to favor the custodial parent regarding a child's religious upbringing, but we're seeing a shift in this area. I represented a man, a soldier who fought in Afghanistan, who was in the process of divorce; he is Catholic and his ex is not. When he said he wanted to have their infant son baptized, she objected. Ultimately the court decided in my client's favor, and he was allowed to have his son baptized, as well as continue exposing him to other Catholic practices and traditions. Increasingly the courts consider it important that both parents in interfaith marriages have something to say about a child's religion after the divorce.

Similarly, let your lawyer know if you're being excluded from health care decisions or school activities. These can be red flags that signal a more systematic exclusion from the life of your child. If you tell your attorney about the specifics of the exclusion, she may be able to design a strategy to prevent this from happening. For instance, when moms and dads have joint legal custody, they are in theory supposed to make all decisions about a child's health care together. Yet a dad might learn after the fact that his child was admitted to the hospital. Or moms don't inform dads about doctors' appointments, medical tests, and the like. Or dads find out that their child is taking a controversial drug and they were not consulted about the prescription.

In terms of school activities, tell your lawyer if you learn that you haven't been informed that your child is participating in soccer, that he received a detention or suspension, or that his teacher requested a parent conference. Also tell him if the stepfather had gone to school events that you weren't informed about, adding insult to injury.

It's also important to inform your attorney if the mom has prohibited your child from contacting you. Unless there is a specific court prohibition against contact between a father and his child (which would be unusual), your son or daughter should feel free to phone, text, or e-mail you at any time. You and your child may be victims of exclusion. For example, the child's mom may have forbidden her from communicating with you except on visitation days; she may have told your child (falsely) that the court prohibits any contact except on those days. Or she may have made up a reason about why your child can't talk to you—that you're too busy or too worn out from work to talk at night. In these situations, don't give up hope. A competent attorney has an excellent chance of restoring your legal rights in most circumstances.

Understand That Your Parenting Time Is a Protected Right

The law protects your parenting time and visitation rights. In every state, a custodial parent can be cited for civil contempt for interfering with parenting time or visitation. As the coauthor of an Illinois law that criminalizes such interference, I am acutely aware that many divorced dads don't realize this law exists, and so they often give up and assume it's not worth it to contact their attorney when their child's mom does these things:

- Reduces the amount of court-ordered visitation time they spend with their kids (reduces it randomly or consistently)
- Supervises some or all of the time spent with a child (even when there is no court-ordered supervision)
- Insists that the stepfather or boyfriend share or split the visitation time with you
- Dictates what you can and cannot do during visitation periods

In some states, you don't have to contact a lawyer to enforce your rights, at least in theory. When interference with parenting time and visitation is criminalized, you have only to make a complaint to the police. If the police don't provide the assistance you need, that's when to contact a lawyer for help.

Capitalize on the Options the Law Gives You

The law gives you a number of potential remedies if you feel you are being pushed out of your children's lives. One option is to file a petition for change of custody and a motion for an in camera interview of your children by the judge (this is an interview in the privacy of the judge's chambers) if you believe your ex and her partner are wrongfully interfering with your court-ordered visitation and attempting to push you out of the child's life. If the children are old enough to communicate effectively, the judge may interview them and ask them about what their mom and their stepfather said or did. Be aware, however, that noncustodial parents are at a disadvantage in these situations because custodial parents generally have access to the children prior to the interview with the judge and can coach them as to what they should say.

Therefore, you may need to avail yourself of option 2: a psychological or psychiatric evaluation of your kids. A sharp, well-qualified mental health professional often can spot the signs of parental alienation. If the children have been told or encouraged to choose a stepfather over you—if your ex has been saying that you're not as good a parent as her new husband or has embarked on a campaign to brainwash your kids (demonstrating that they owe you neither respect nor loyalty)—a savvy therapist can ask the questions and evaluate the answers that help identify this strategy.

You also have the option of appearing in court, and in some instances, this is enough to convince a judge to order your ex (and the boyfriend or stepfather) to refrain from bad-mouthing you. Some moms are so furious at their ex-husbands that they can't control what they say about him in front of the children or even in court. Typically this type of angry mom has called you bad names in front of the children and accused you of "crimes" you never committed. She knows that the kids have witnessed this repeated behavior, as have others, and so when she appears in court, she often confirms this behavior rather than lie about it. She is aware there are too many witnesses to her behavior for her to get caught committing perjury and potentially ending up incarcerated.

Joint Custody and a Good Divorce Agreement Are Your Best Protection

This should be the first point rather than the fourth, but by the time you're reading this book, you may already be divorced. Still, I urge you to review your divorce agreement and look at what it says about your legal rights concerning issues such as school activities, religion, and Father's Day. If the agreement is a good one, it should contain highly specific language about your rights regarding these and other matters if they are the source of potential conflict. The less specific the language is, the easier it is for a mom and a stepfather to conspire against you and rob you of time you and your kids deserve with each other. At our firm, we ask all clients to fill out a highly detailed questionnaire before we begin working on their case. One of our goals is to anticipate areas of potential conflict and make sure they're addressed in the divorce agreement.

Similarly, joint custody should afford dads more decision-making control in their child's life, and this helps diminish the possibility that your ex can kick you to the curb. Even if you lack a joint custody arrangement, however, the courts still protect the basic rights of biological fathers, especially when those fathers are involved with their kids and adhering to an agreement's visitation and support provisions.

Engage Rather Than Withdraw

Here are some of the reasons divorced dads give about why their children are better off spending time with stepfathers rather than themselves:

- "He has a lot more money than I do. He can give the kids a better place to live, send them to a nice private school, buy them the toys they want. That's why I know they prefer him to me."

- "My ex married a guy who is a lot more warm and fuzzy than I am. He's great with the kids and I'm more reserved, so the kids respond to him better."

- "My children's stepfather spends a lot more time with them than I do because they live with him and my ex. They get along great with him, and when I come for my visitation time, my kids have a hard time warming up to me. It's like I'm a stranger."

Many divorced dads are victims of the myth of the stepfather. They come to believe that because these second dads are with their kids a lot or because they have more money or charm, they forge stronger bonds with the children. Although it may appear that way from a divorced dad's perspective, it rarely is true. Study after study has demonstrated that the biological bond generally trumps all others. Instinctively when they're young and cognitively when they're older, kids see themselves as their dads. Not only are the mannerisms and expressions similar between you and your kids but so too are your interests and abilities. As long as dads make a consistent effort to be present in their children's lives, they will have an advantage over every other male parental figure.

The relationship between stepparents and stepchildren has been studied extensively, and researchers have concluded that many problems exist in this relationship—more than between biological parents and their children. Here are some key findings:

- "Stepparents do not, on average, love their children as much as genetic parents, and are more likely than genetic parents to feel indifference or hostility toward their children."[1]
- "Biological fathers score higher on measures of parental warmth and control compared to stepfathers."[2]
- "In a study using a national probability sample of 1,250 fathers of school-aged children, it was found that stepfathers spent less time with children than fathers in family structures where there are two biological parents."[3]

All this isn't to say that stepdads can't be good parents. As I noted at the beginning of the chapter, some stepfathers assume the role of psychological parent and do an excellent job. My point here is that if you're a biological father, you should remind yourself that no matter how strongly you believe that your role is being usurped, you have significant advantages over a stepfather when it comes to forming and sustaining relationships with your kids. This reminder will help prevent you from doing what some divorced dads do when confronted with what they feel is a "superior" step-father: withdraw.

This isn't a gender-specific reaction; it happens to both divorced dads and moms, though usually for different reasons. Typically when moms are the custodial parent, they reach a point of anger and frustration (often when the kids are teenagers) because they're the ones spending the most time taking care of the kids. When they've had it—when they say they want dad to take the kids for a while—they usually communicate the follow-ing sentiment: "I want you to see what it's like to take care of the kids 24/7, to help them with their homework, to wash their dirty clothes, to listen to their smart mouths."

With dads, the catalyst for withdrawal is often the new stepfather or boyfriend. Typically their withdrawal happens incre-mentally rather than immediately. They see that the stepdad is going to be around one weekend, and so they miss that visitation period. They hear their son bragging about the stepdad's prowess at baseball, and they skip another visitation or end it prematurely. When the family moves into the stepfather's fancy house, the biological dad finds his self-esteem bottoming out, and he misses more time with his kids.

What's even worse is that biological dads rationalize this with-drawal. Rather than face the fact that they're deserting the peo-ple in the world who need them the most, they make excuses for themselves. Here's one excuse that I've heard frequently: "She's only five now, and her mom and stepdad really control things since that's who she is with all the time. But when my kid turns eighteen, she'll be out from under their control and can live with me then. By that point, she'll realize why I divorced her mom. Right now, my ex has brainwashed our daughter into believing that her new husband walks on water. She'll see the truth when she's older, though, and I'll reestablish my relationship with her at that point." By then it may be too late. Your estrangement will likely be permanent after years of absence or even partial absence. Yet I recognize that the impulse to withdraw in the face of what seems to be unfair paternal competition is strong. To fight against that impulse, the best thing you can do is communicate with your children. When you perceive that they are favoring the stepdad or boyfriend over you or make unflattering comparisons that hurt you ("Our stepfather lets us watch that program. He's a lot nicer than you!"), make an effort to talk with them from the heart.

How you communicate depends on their ages. For younger children (under the age of five), reassure them that no matter what your mother might have told them, you'll always be there for them. Many times dads hear from their kids that their mom said that he won't be around much "but your stepfather will be here." This is frightening to toddlers and kids who haven't started school. When they ask you if their stepfather is going to be their new dad or if you still love them, it will break your heart. But if you can reassure them that you're always going to be there for them and back that up with consistent, present behavior, they'll stop being frightened that you'll disappear. Just as important, you'll feel better about yourself and your place in their lives when they stop asking you these types of questions.

With children ages six to twelve, as with younger children, you should not denigrate their mom (even if she has denigrated you as a dad). At this age, the kids are still too young for you to be completely open and honest about how your feelings were hurt by something they said or did. But you can point out the bond that connects you with them—that even though the stepfather may be rich or lenient, you will always be part of their lives. Explain to them why you insist they have to go to bed at a certain time when they stay at your house or why you're unable to afford to buy them everything that their stepdad buys. Don't be defensive in your explanation or negative about the stepfather. Just let them know the truth. They'll feel better, and so will you.

With adolescents, you can be more open and honest. If they said or did something that's bothering you, address it. Don't accuse them of being mean or of taking their mom's or stepfather's side. Be straightforward about how you feel, and tell them if you're disappointed in how they acted. Although they may not acknowledge your disappointment and hurt, they'll understand that you care enough about them to level with them. It will make them think twice about repeating the offending behavior.

Finally, be aware that if you withdraw rather than communicate and engage, the only real victim is your child. Demarcus learned this the hard way. After his divorce from Yvette, he saw his eleven-year-old son, Carlos, regularly for two years. When Yvette remarried, however, Demarcus found it more difficult to be with Carlos. Part of the problem was that he had been downsized out of a job, while Yvette's new husband was the senior vice president of a Fortune 100 company; he felt diminished in his son's eyes. Another part of the problem was that Carlos was just starting to go through adolescence, and he was acting out a lot, especially when Demarcus was around. Carlos was well aware that his father felt diminished by his stepfather's success and he was quick to point out his stepdad's strengths versus Demarcus's weaknesses.

Although Demarcus continued to make his support payments, he didn't see Carlos as often as he might have. When he found a new job, he used work as an excuse for missing a number of visitation days and events at Carlos's school. Later, when Demarcus remarried and had two kids, he rationalized that his new family commitments prevented him from spending as much time with Carlos as he wanted to. Even when he did do something with Carlos, Demarcus rarely opened up with him. Instead, they would spend time together eating meals or watching television but rarely talking about their feelings. Demarcus was always wary of comparisons with Carlos's stepfather and so kept their conversations on safe ground.

While it seemed to Demarcus that Carlos had turned out okay—he had gotten past his adolescent rebelliousness, was accepted at an excellent college, and is now a young lawyer—he has been in therapy since college. He struggles to form relationships with both men and women, a problem not only in his career but in his personal life—he complains a lot about being lonely.

While it's impossible to know if Demarcus's withdrawal from his son's life caused these relationship problems, they no doubt contributed to them.

I hope this story serves as a cautionary tale if you're thinking about withdrawing from your kids' lives. It doesn't matter who a stepfather is or if he is enormously smart, successful, empathetic, and wealthy. Psychologically, your kids need the consistent presence and emotional involvement of their biological dad. If you make yourself scarce because you feel you don't measure up to their stepfather or you allow your ex to push you away, you may be condemning your kids to a lifetime of psychotherapy or worse. If you overcome your doubts and fears and maintain the relationship with your children, you give them a much better shot at a successful adulthood.

CHAPTER 7

Therapy Isn't for Women Only

Dealing with Your Issues So You Can Have a Better Relationship with Your Kids

"I'm not crazy. It's my wife who should be seeing a shrink."

Variations on this statement are common. When lawyers, mediators, or judges mention therapy, divorcing dads are generally resistant. Many times, dads are convinced that if they enter therapy, judges will view them as emotionally unbalanced and it will hurt their chances of getting the custody arrangement or visitation they want. In other instances, they resist therapy because they believe that it's what their wife wants and they're not going to give her the satisfaction of winning on this point. And in a surprisingly large number of cases, dads hold the traditional male view of therapy as being only for the weak: going to therapy is not the macho thing to do.

I hope this chapter will demonstrate how harmful these beliefs are, not only to you but to your children. Good divorced dads make the effort to do everything possible to be better parents, and therapy can help in many ways. It can help men deal with their feelings and be better parents to their children, and it can help them deal with the emotional turmoil that a divorce creates. Divorce is a crucible, and anyone who has been through a contested divorce with battles over custody and visitation knows how traumatic the process can be for both parents. Women are more inclined to deal with this trauma through therapy, develop a strong emotional support network, and express their feelings. Men often resist therapy, frequently lack a strong emotional support network, and are loathe to express their feelings. Thus, they often are a mess during and after a divorce, and many times, this state hurts their legal strategy—they lack objectivity and make bad decisions, damaging their legal case—as well as their relationship to their children. Therapy can help you obtain a degree of objectivity that's crucial for a favorable legal outcome and a better postdivorce relationship with your kids.

Several types of therapy fit within the unfolding divorce process.

From Family Therapy to Anger Management

Before, during, and after the divorce, men have various options for help under the therapy umbrella, including these:

- One-on-one counseling with a trained therapist—a social worker, psychologist, or psychiatrist
- Coaching with life coaches who are certified as such and may also be social workers, psychologists, or psychiatrists
- Support groups, from therapy sessions with men and women to ones specifically for divorcing or divorced dads
- Anger management, often conducted by a therapist
- Parenting classes
- Family therapy in which all family members participate
- Marriage counseling

When dads take advantage of these options depends on a variety of factors. Certainly men can opt to go into therapy or join a support group at any point. Here, though, are the common entry points:

- *As part of the mediation process.* A mediator recommends that parents become involved in some type of therapy to help them resolve their differences about custody, visitation, or some other issue.
- *As a result of a motion.* For instance, the wife's attorney files a motion requesting a psychological evaluation. Though the evaluation isn't therapy, it's usually conducted by a therapist and can lead to some form of counseling.
- *As a response to a child advocate's recommendation.* The court may appoint a child advocate or representative (different states have different names) to represent the interests of a child during the divorce. This advocate may find that the child is being adversely affected by arguments between the dad and mom and recommend both go into therapy.
- *As a result of a third-party request.* Typically this third party is the school a child attends. Teachers see the child behaving in ways that are disturbing. Maybe he's acting out in school or seems depressed. This behavior coincides with the divorce proceeding, and they contact the court (directly or indirectly) and a recommendation for therapy (for the father, mother, and the child) is recommended.
- *As part of the divorce agreement.* The judge orders therapy for both parents.

In considering the precipitating events of therapy and the kinds of therapy, understand that the courts are not generally concerned with your or your wife's depression, self-esteem, and anger unless it is having a serious, negative impact on your children. Therefore, they will not order therapy in most cases without a good cause related to your kids. A mediator may recommend it to help you deal with thorny custody or visitation problems, but the mediator's recommendation isn't binding. It's up to you and your wife to follow through with it.

Second, a judge will probably not suggest therapy just because one spouse complains that the other spouse is being difficult. The courts need a compelling reason to order therapy. A bipolar disorder, serious abuse allegations, or neglect of a child are just some examples where courts might believe that therapy is necessary.

Third, when therapy is recommended, it is usually recommended for both parents and not just one. In fact, if you file a motion asking that your wife be ordered to attend therapy sessions, you will probably find that the court wants you to attend them as well, especially if this motion is made before the divorce is final. The courts like to be even-handed in these matters prior to the divorce.

The larger issue is what you get out of therapy. If you go into it believing it won't help and you therefore passively or actively resist a therapist's questions and suggestions, the experience will be worthless. To encourage you to take advantage of this resource, I'd like to provide you with some compelling evidence of its value.

What You Should Know About Therapy and Divorce

I've alluded to how therapy helps divorcing dads with both their emotional challenges and legal issues. Let's look at the emotional aspect first.

According to Dr. Alan Childs, a psychologist with whom our firm works, divorce hits dads especially hard because they're often not as adept as moms at acknowledging and expressing their feelings. "It's one of the first times in their marital lives when they have to deal with loss," he said. "Their ego is fractured, and they're feeling helpless. They fear that they'll lose their kids or at least their connection with them. They can experience a psychological downward spiral in which they feel anxious, agitated, depressed, and scared."

In this stage, it's difficult to be a good divorced dad. You may be feeling so badly about yourself that you don't want to see your kids because you're ashamed: you feel you've let them down because your behavior was responsible for ending the marriage or you believe your financial problems (for example, you lost your job and couldn't find another one) were the precipitating cause of the divorce. You also are so fearful of losing your children figuratively and literally that you go into warrior mode. You fight your wife on every single issue, large or small, and turn the divorce into an expensive and emotionally draining experience.

Therapy isn't a panacea for all the intense emotions divorce stirs up, but it does help men deal with these feelings and diminishes the negative behaviors that result from them. A good therapist will talk to men about their most intense emotions and especially about their fears. When Dr. Childs asks his divorcing male patients what they fear most, nine out of ten say they fear they'll lose their children. In the majority of cases, this is an unfounded fear. The therapist, in conjunction with the dad's lawyer, can explain why this fear is groundless—why even if a wife has threatened a dad with this outcome, the courts recognize the value of making sure that both parents stay involved in a child's life. Unless the dad is guilty of some heinous behavior—physical or sexual abuse, drug addiction, criminal activities—then he usually controls whether he remains a good divorced dad.

Many of our clients who have gone through therapy also receive help with their low self-esteem. Therapists help them understand that they should not blame themselves as much as a variety of factors that made divorce inevitable. Many times, it's no one's fault, though each person's behaviors may have accelerated the end of the marriage.

Dan is the father of two boys and a girl, and he and his wife, Marissa, were divorcing after twelve years of marriage. Dan had moved out of the house and had moved in with his elderly mother, who had a small apartment on the other side of the city. Though neither Dan nor his wife was having affairs, their relationship had grown increasingly contentious over the years, and they argued about everything. They had gone to marriage counseling, and it had helped initially, but things soon became worse. Finally, Dan told his wife that he didn't think the marriage was ever going to work and he wanted a divorce.

Over the next few months, Dan's relationship with his kids worsened, in large part because his wife told them that he was the one who was "breaking up the family" and that he was selfish and self-involved and didn't really care about them. Dan's eleven-year-old daughter refused to speak with him. Dan was miserable, in large part because he believed what his wife had said about him. Depressed and feeling guilty, in no small part because he was living with his mother, Dan told his wife that she could have whatever she wanted in a divorce—from the house to sole custody. He said he wasn't hiring a lawyer and would do exactly as she requested.

Before the divorce went through, though, Dan decided to start therapy at the urging of his sister. Relatively quickly, the therapist helped Dan recognize that "it takes two to tango—and two to stop tangoing." She also helped him realize that he had always been a good, involved father and that his kids were reacting to his wife's negative statements about him. It became clear to Dan that though he hadn't been a perfect husband, he had tried to make the marriage work from the start through the end. His willingness to go through marriage counseling was proof of his commitment to it. The therapy helped Dan change his mind about sole custody: he hired a lawyer and had him file for joint custody, which the court granted. Relatively soon after the divorce went through, Dan's relationship with his daughter as well as his two other children improved.

In addition, therapy helps divorcing dads understand what their kids are going through. A three year old, for instance, has attached (psychologically speaking) to his dad, and when his dad moves out, he may become extremely angry—hitting, screaming, crying. Dads need to recognize this behavior for what it is: a natural reaction to the separation of a child from a parent to whom he's attached. Rather than blame themselves, they need to reassure the child that they'll always be there for him.

A sixteen year old may react to a divorce through role confusion. Instead of worrying about what she's going to wear to the school dance and how she can get an A in her toughest class, she's anxious about whether her parents will be able to pay the mortgage next month or how to handle her little sister's anger at their dad or mom. Again, divorcing dads need to talk straight with their adolescents and encourage them to concentrate on adolescent responsibilities, not take on adult roles. If dads feel that their children need additional help, they might want to explore avenues to get their children into therapy. They may want to talk to their own therapist about options, to their ex, to their lawyer, or to their kids' counselors at school.

Making a Stronger Case for Yourself as a Parent

Ask divorce attorneys who their most difficult client is and they'll respond, "A litigant I can't control." These clients exhibit a variety of behaviors and make a number of bad choices that adversely affect their cases. Although their lawyers tell them they must remain calm before a hearing in front of the judge, the heated exchanges, baiting, and emotionally provocative questions can cause them to respond angrily and in other inappropriate ways.

Some divorcing dads laugh mockingly or accuse their spouse of lying when they're accused of something false. Other dads make facial gestures—grimacing, eye-rolling, smirking—that communicates their disbelief and disgust. Still others blow up: they have temper tantrums during a hearing.

All of this is understandable but likely to prejudice a judge against them. The judge figures that if they can't control themselves in court, they can't control themselves when they are with their children. These uncontrolled behaviors cause judges to suspect that the false charges they're reacting so strongly against may in fact be true. Why else would they be putting on such an inappropriate show in court?

Beyond these negative behaviors displayed in front of a judge, divorcing dads can also mess up their cases in other ways. Perhaps the most common is to become so focused on seeking accountability that they lose sight of what they and their children require. They rationalize to themselves that they are doing the right thing, but many times, they are not protecting their relationship with the children. They are so furious at the unconscionable demands of their spouse as part of the divorce settlement that they go ballistic and take the bait. They may become paranoid and believe that their spouse is engaging in parental alienation when that isn't what she's doing. As a result, divorcing dads decide they must wage an all-out war, no matter the cost. Their desire is to tell their side of the story in court, to explain why and how their wife is behaving so badly.

In essence, they're using the courtroom as the couch. Therapy, however, not the courtroom, is for venting. Although therapy may not be cheap, it's still far less expensive than using a courtroom to get your feelings out in the open.

The flip side is responding incorrectly to the divorce with extreme passivity rather than extreme aggressiveness. Either way, these men are allowing their emotions—emotions that could have been dealt with in therapy—to influence decisions about the divorce settlement that will probably haunt them for years to come.

You should also be aware that if you have had legal problems in the past—from alcoholism, drugs, or physical abuse, for example—the court will probably look more favorably on your parenting requests if you've started therapy voluntarily to manage these problems. For example, if someone whose wife has called the police because he threatened her makes a good-faith effort to attend anger management classes, the judge will often trust that he is sincere in his desire to control his anger and be a good parent. Or if the father is depressed and neglectful, his willingness to work through these issues with a therapist demonstrates that he's making an effort. Remember that the courts usually want both parents to be involved in raising their child, and they try to be optimistic that dads as well as moms will get whatever help they need to become better parents. If you make a commitment to therapy, therefore, a judge is more likely to see it as you making a commitment to your child.

For all these reasons, consider whether therapy might help you as a person, a parent, and from a legal perspective. Talk to your attorney about these issues. Don't avoid this subject because you believe therapy will be prohibitively expensive; don't tell yourself that you'll do it later, after the divorce, when you have one less major thing on your plate. At the very least, being in therapy will help you view the divorce process with greater objectivity. Once you've had the chance to express your anger, fears, sadness, disappointment, and other powerful feelings, they tend to have less of a hold on your mind. Just taking the edge off these strong emotions can give you enough space to weigh your legal options with greater clarity. You won't make a decision to give up custody because you feel guilty. You won't agree to unfair visitation provisions because your self-esteem is so low you can't muster the energy to contest these provisions. You won't use the divorce process as a cudgel to punish your wife for real and imagined sins and leave your children emotionally vulnerable when they witness the resulting acrimony for months or years to come.

How to Find and Benefit from a Therapist

You may never have been in therapy before the divorce and haven't a clue about how to find the right therapist. You probably have a lot of questions about the process: what type of therapist is best, how you can you find someone who is knowledgeable about dads and divorce, and so on. The process isn't that complicated, but I've learned through experience that certain search techniques are more effective than others, as well as which specific attitudes and actions will help you get the most out of therapy. Let's focus first on the search. Here are three steps that help divorcing dads find the right therapist:

- *Ask your lawyer for a referral.* Surprisingly, many men never think to ask their lawyers for a therapist referral, perhaps because they see the two professions as completely separate. In reality, a good divorce lawyer has at least one therapist to recommend to clients, since it's such a common need. Our firm has a number of therapists we recommend for clients based on their specific needs.

- *Make sure the therapist has a great deal of experience working with divorcing dads.* Many don't. That's because many more women are in therapy than men. As this book makes clear, your situation and issues are different in many ways from those that your wife is facing. Therefore, you need a therapist who recognizes that many dads have self-esteem issues when going through a divorce and that many of these men equate financial worth with self-worth. They also are attuned to the struggles dads have with their kids in noncustodial parenting roles.

- *Talk to another divorcing dad who has been a patient of a possible therapist.* Your prospective therapist probably won't be willing to give you the name of another patient because of confidentiality issues, but if you get a referral from your lawyer, she may be willing to ask her client if he would talk to you about his therapist. In this way, you can gain insights into the process, and you may be motivated to seek help because this other individual will tell you how the therapist helped him deal with a variety of situations.

As important as it is to find a therapist, it's equally important to go into therapy with the right attitude and to monitor the initial sessions. Specifically, do the following:

- *Resolve to be open about your feelings—your fears and hopes.* If you go into therapy figuring you'll just tell the therapist what he wants to hear, the sessions will be a waste of time. Whether it's your fear of losing the connection with your kids or your desire for accountability based on your wife's bad behavior, you have to verbalize these feelings. I know this is difficult for divorcing dads who may have a great deal on their mind, but your openness can help you as a dad and help your lawyer achieve a favorable outcome.

- *Be alert for gender bias or other negative therapist attitudes*. Sad
  to say, some therapists are gender biased. Unfortunately,
  you may not discover this fact until you're in a session with
  one of them and this person says something or asks you a
  question that betrays this bias. For instance, the therapist
  may suggest that your wife may be able to handle being a
  parent better than you and you should consider not seeking
  joint custody. It's also possible that the therapist will be more
  subtle in displays of gender bias; his or her expressions and
  comments might make you feel even more guilty about the
  marriage's failure and your self-esteem plummets further.

If you feel that your therapist has a gender bias that is interfering with the therapy, don't be afraid to find another one and
inform your attorney immediately. Ideally, if you follow the previous three steps, you increase the odds that you'll find the right
therapist for a divorcing dad.

Specific Situations: Tailoring Your Tactics

Situations vary when it comes to divorce and therapy. If you're
facing therapy because of abuse allegations versus therapy for you
and your wife because you can't agree about a visitation schedule,
your situations are different. Similarly, your kids may be ordered
into therapy by a judge, and you need to understand why this order
is made and what it entails.

To that end, review these common situations and some issues
that may came up and how to deal with them:

- *Abuse or neglect allegations*. If you or your spouse files a motion
  alleging abuse or neglect during the divorce process, the
  court may order one or both of you into therapy. Typically
  you could each see a different therapist. A psychological
  evaluation could be part of this process, conducted by yet
  another therapist. If serious allegations of this type are filed

against you, you probably will not be able to see your children until these allegations are resolved or you won't be able to see them without supervision. Be aware that as a man, you're particularly vulnerable to false allegations as part of a concocted divorce legal strategy, especially if a paper trail exists that gives credence to these allegations—say, the police were called to your residence to resolve a domestic disturbance or your wife filed charges against you for anything from verbal threats to physical abuse.

- *Mediation*. If you're in mediation as part of the legal process, the mediator may recommend therapy for you or your wife, but you're not bound by this recommendation unless the judge orders it (at least in most states). Still, the mediator's recommendation carries weight with judges, and if you and your wife are unable to resolve your differences through mediation, it probably is wise from a personal as well as a legal standpoint to follow the recommendation. Mediators may recommend a therapist or tell you to consult your attorney for a referral. Therapy to resolve these types of disputes tends to be short term and usually ends when the issues are resolved.

- A *child advocate's recommendation*. Child advocates or representatives are appointed for a variety of reasons. You may learn that your spouse's new boyfriend, who has been spending a lot of time with the children, is a drug dealer, and you file a motion that includes the appointment of a child representative to protect them from the influences of the boyfriend. It's also possible that a child representative is appointed because the child's school notices that your son or daughter is depressed or exhibiting other alarming behavioral changes during the divorce process, and they inform the court of these issues. Or it may be that the constant and heated verbal arguments in front of the kids has taken a toll, and a child representative is appointed to help the child deal with what he has witnessed. These child representatives often recommend that the kids see a therapist to help them work through their feelings about the divorce.

- *A judge's recognition that kids need help.* Judges can peremptorily order therapeutic intervention if they believe kids are in trouble or would benefit from seeing a therapist. Though many judges would prefer to wait for mediation to take place and visitation and custody issues to be resolved, they may find that children need emotional help immediately (for example, because they're depressed or acting out in some way, or there's evidence of physical harm) and can issue that order.

Here are a few other situational variables. First, although the courts act swiftly to get kids help if they believe the children are suffering or in danger, they move relatively slowly when it comes to therapy orders for adults. Typically a motion has to be made and a hearing has to be held before a therapy order is entered, and weeks or months can elapse before the order is issued. Even after it's issued, the courts will usually provide you or your spouse time to find a therapist who is appropriate; you're also given time to find someone who accepts your type of insurance.

Second, in general, don't expect a divorce decree that will order your wife to undergo therapy for the next two years or some other extended period of time. The courts are not in the mental health business. They expect you and your spouse to take responsibility for dealing with your own issues, and when they order therapy, it is usually to protect the children or help you and your spouse resolve problems that are making it difficult for you to reach an agreement about custody and visitation.

Third, therapy recommendations vary by state. The courts in some states are much quicker to recommend or order parents or kids into therapy than others, and they have different rules about how many sessions are necessary for a given issue or problem.

Self-Assessment: Can Therapy Help You?

Most men going through a divorce have a hard time answering this question objectively. If you're there or have been there, you know exactly what I mean. You're either so angry and upset about the divorce that you can't think clearly about this issue or you're so depressed that you lack the motivational energy to find and see a therapist. Yet as an attorney who has represented countless, angry, confused, and depressed divorcing dads, I cannot overemphasize the need to reach out to a therapist despite your doubts about its efficacy. Therapy can make a huge difference not only in terms of the outcome of the divorce but in the relationship you have with your kids for years to come.

Joel found himself blinded by rage when his wife, Georgia, filed for a divorce. Georgia had been having an affair with her boss, and when she told Joel that she loved her boss and not him, he was furious. He became even angrier when Georgia informed him that she would be seeking sole custody of their six-year-old son. When Joel became our client, he made it clear that he wanted sole custody himself and was prepared and eager for us to litigate the divorce so he could get on the public record all the things that Georgia had done that he considered "evil." One of his points of emphasis was that he wanted us to use Georgia's conviction for selling marijuana against her, even though it had occurred years before Joel had met her. Though he hadn't told his son about this conviction, he maintained that he wanted to have an official document that he could show his son when he was older to demonstrate that Georgia, rather than himself, had broken up the family.

It was clear to us that Joel not only was not thinking clearly about what he wanted the divorce to accomplish but that he wasn't thinking about his best interest and that of his child. We convinced him to see a therapist, who concurred that Joel was in tremendous pain and that it was coming out as hostility and a desire for accountability. We had talked to Joel about how he was an excellent candidate for joint custody and that sole custody was unlikely, but he had been adamant about pursuing his original goal. After a number of therapy sessions, however, Joel began to consider his other options. He was still extremely angry at Georgia, but the therapy helped him take a step back and consider what was best for him and his son. He began to understand the importance of crafting a legal strategy that stood the best chance of ensuring he'd be a regular part of his son's life. He also understood that all the money that he wanted to spend humiliating his wife through extended litigation would be better spent on his son's future.

It took a number of conversations with the therapist and with lawyers at our firm, but Joel finally relented and agreed to try and reach a settlement, as well as seek joint rather than sole custody. We were able to hammer out a fair settlement and also joint custody, and everyone who worked on this case at our firm knew that it would not have been possible without the assistance of a therapist.

I hope this story inspires you to answer the following questions, which will help you assess whether a therapist might help you achieve your parenting and legal objectives:

1. Do you find it difficult to enjoy any activity because you're overcome by feelings of anger related to the divorce?

2. Do you direct all your conversations with friends and family back to the divorce?

3. Have you lost your job (or feel you're in danger of losing it) because you can't concentrate to do the work effectively?

4. Have you become extremely lethargic and feel as if you don't have the energy to contest the divorce terms (even if you feel they're unfair to you and to your children)?

5. Are you so depressed by the divorce that you've decided not to hire an attorney and are representing yourself at the hearing?

6. Are you arguing constantly with your wife about every single aspect of the divorce, from who gets the ice trays to custody issues?

7. Do you find yourself fantasizing frequently about escaping— about leaving town, never seeing your children again, and starting fresh?

8. Do you beat yourself up about the failure of the marriage? Do you tell yourself that your wife and kids will be better off without you?

9. Are you unable to agree with your attorney about a course of legal action? Have you found yourself repeatedly telling him that you want to ignore his advice and pursue your own objectives?

10. Do you find yourself relying on drugs or alcohol (or both) to deal with the divorce?

If you responded yes to any of these questions, ask yourself follow-up questions regarding the frequency and intensity. In other words, how often do you behave in this way, and how intensely do you feel? For instance, in response to question 8, you might reply, "I beat up on myself about the failure of the marriage all the time and have said to just about everyone I know that my children will be better off without me. I feel this way to the bottom of my soul."

If you answered yes to at least two questions and your follow-up frequency and intensity are high, then you should discuss with your attorney the possible benefits of therapy. If your attorney agrees that you would benefit from it, don't delay getting help. Recognize that your window of opportunity for action can be closing; a pivotal hearing in the divorce process can occur in weeks or even earlier, but it may take you a number of sessions with a therapist until you can think critically and objectively about your options. As a general rule, the sooner you start therapy, the better the outcome will be for you and your children.

CHAPTER 8

Legal Remedies

*How the Courts Can Help
You and Your Kids*

Throughout the previous chapters, I've discussed the legal process and how divorcing dads can use it effectively to achieve positive outcomes for themselves and their kids. Here I focus on a few crucial legal strategies and issues for divorcing dads. More specifically, I detail the common misconceptions that surround these legal subjects, as well as how to use the law throughout your divorce to improve your relationship with your kids.

This chapter isn't meant to take the place of your own lawyer but to make you an educated consumer so you know the questions to ask and the goals to strive for. It also may provide information that your attorney may neglect to discuss. Divorce attorneys generally know the letter of the law, but what concerns me—and what I believe will concern you—goes beyond the statutes. You must know how father-child relationships are affected by divorce law and how the specific custody and visitation provisions you agree to can have a positive or negative effect on your kids.

Knowledge is power, and ideally this knowledge will help you become an active participant in the legal process and enable you to help your attorney craft the best strategy possible. It isn't what you know that can hurt you but what you don't know.

The Joint Custody Misconception

As you probably know by now, I'm a strong advocate of joint custody. As the coauthor of the Illinois Joint Custody Act, I've spent a lot of time studying the subject from both parenting and legal perspectives. I cannot overemphasize how important joint custody is for many divorcing dads—how it provides for the collaborative parental decision making that not only increases the odds that dads will be active participants in their children's lives but decreases the odds of future legal battles because dads were excluded from key decisions.

You would think that most dads would ask for joint custody, but this often isn't the case. That's because they suffer from the common misconception that it's difficult, if not impossible, for men to get joint custody if their spouse is resisting this arrangement.

While obstacles to joint custody do exist, dads have a decent shot at getting joint custody, assuming that they don't have a history that would cause a judge to be skeptical about their parenting commitment or their character. For instance, if a father hasn't seen his child for many years because he decided he wanted to travel, if he abuses drugs or alcohol, or if he has criminal convictions pertaining to domestic violence, then joint custody is unlikely. Most divorcing dads, however, assume they don't have a shot at joint custody for these reasons:

- The legal system is gender biased.
- Their state laws favor sole custody for moms.
- Winning the legal battle for joint custody is prohibitively expensive and time-consuming.

- Their lack of self-esteem convinces them that the kids would be better off if the mom has sole custody.

I'm not suggesting that these reasons aren't obstacles. I'm also not suggesting that you can't be a good divorced dad when moms have sole custody (and I'll set out the legal strategies for noncustodial parents later in the chapter). What I want you to realize is that you shouldn't automatically cede custody to the mom for these reasons. You need to talk to your lawyer about whether joint custody is feasible, and the discussion should start with an evaluation of the factors that influence courts' custody decisions, including these:

- *You and your spouse's preferences.* In the vast majority of cases, if you and your spouse agree on a custody arrangement, the court will approve it. Your arrangement can be traditional: mom retains physical custody, but you both share in major decisions regarding your child. Or your arrangement can be untraditional: dad has physical custody or you and your spouse alternately reside in one house where the kids consistently live (what is known as a "nesting arrangement"). The courts will disregard your mutual wishes only if they feel they're not in the best interest of the kids.
- *Environmental stability.* The courts recognize that divorce is often a highly disruptive event in kids' lives, and they want to do everything possible to maintain an emotionally secure existence for them. Therefore, they favor custody arrangements that achieve this objective rather than those that seem to create more instability. For this reason, a judge who feels that parents cannot agree about anything will be reluctant to grant joint custody, based on the assumption that their constant verbal battles will be harmful to the children.
- *Violence.* The courts will do everything possible to avoid placing a child in the custody of any parent who has a history of violence—convictions for battery or domestic violence,

for instance. Although they may be swayed by arguments and evidence that this spouse has been rehabilitated, it often is a difficult factor to overcome for the formerly violent parent.

- *Mental and physical health.* This pertains to both the kids and the parents. In the former case, the courts look at who can best take care of a disabled child, for instance. The courts may also determine if a given parent has a disability that might prevent him or her from taking care of a child adequately.

- *Lifestyle.* This is probably the most variable factor, since one judge may find nothing wrong with a given lifestyle, while another might find it detrimental to a child. Years ago, for instance, courts in certain parts of the country might have frowned on a parent who was gay and rejected joint or sole custody on this ground. Today the most common lifestyle criteria concern work. Is the parent traveling constantly and physically unable to participate consistently in a child's upbringing?

Many other factors can enter into custody decisions, from the preferences of older children, to the emotional relationship of a child and parent, to the financial resources of each parent. But these five areas are the ones likely to be applicable to most situations. It's great if you and your wife can agree on joint custody and everything proceeds smoothly from that agreement. I suspect, however, that many of divorcing dads are not this lucky. Instead, you may be thinking that joint custody would be good, but your wife wants sole custody. Let's also assume that you're a relatively typical couple: neither you nor your spouse has a history of domestic violence or any criminal convictions, you both enjoy good physical and mental health, you both have normal lifestyles, and you both can provide environmental stability.

When you're seeking joint custody and your wife is resisting, you need to know some inside information about how joint custody decisions are really made and what you can do to influence the outcome to benefit you and your children.

Mediation, Negotiation, and Location

Start out by understanding the reason or reasons your wife is opposed to joint custody. Perhaps she's angry with you and blames you for the failure of the marriage, and she wants to punish you by denying you joint custody. Perhaps she's worried that joint custody will be untenable because you argued so much during the marriage that you're bound to argue even more after it. Or perhaps she was inclined to agree with your request for joint custody but her lawyer convinced her that "giving in" immediately was bad legal strategy.

You need to share whatever information you have concerning your wife's reasons for denying joint custody with your attorney so he or she can craft a strategy. Here are some options.

Mediate Without the Interference of Lawyers

I don't mean to denigrate my profession, but some divorce attorneys are more concerned about winning a case for their client than doing what's right for the children. If a mom comes to them and tells them that she's not sure about conceding joint custody to her husband, these lawyers may discourage her from doing so. They'll tell her that she should use this as her trump card in negotiations, refusing to give him joint custody unless he pays her additional support and other monies or gives her the house or makes some other concession.

As a matter of principle, lawyers are argumentative, and even those who are concerned about the welfare of their client's children may inadvertently escalate tensions between their client and her husband, encouraging fighting to the death on every piece of property, visitation proposal, and so on.

Mediation can be an opportunity to discuss custody arrangements without the presence of attorneys. In many geographical areas throughout the country, they are expressly forbidden from being present during these sessions. Instead, a mediator conducts the meetings. A good mediator facilitates discussion and compromise without any gender bias or personal agenda. I've found that if a couple is reasonable, these mediation sessions can shift attitudes significantly from combat to settlement.

Maria and Roberto were divorcing after seven years of marriage and have one child, five-year-old Inez. When the mediation sessions started, Maria had been adamant about fighting joint custody. Roberto had an affair that had precipitated the end of the marriage, and though he had apologized and wanted to try to save the marriage, Maria said it was over and that if it was up to her, she'd never let him see Inez again.

When they met, the mediator began asking her some questions: "What kind of a relationship do you think Roberto has with Inez? How do you think it would affect your daughter if she never got to see him again, or if she saw him infrequently? Has Roberto ever given you any evidence that he's not a sincere and dedicated father?"

The mediator also asked Roberto questions: "How involved do you want to be in Inez's daily life? What values do you hope to impart to her as a father? How do you think joint custody will benefit Inez?"

Through these questions, the mediator was able to show Maria that despite her husband's mistakes in their marriage, he had always been a good father. Perhaps more important, he helped Maria see that she should not punish Inez for her father's mistakes. Although Maria was still furious with Roberto and demanded a lot in the settlement, she relented on the custody issue.

Find a Trade-Off That Might Be Workable

I had a client whose wife was refusing to budge on the issue of joint custody. As we negotiated the issue, my client's wife said to her attorney, "I'll give him joint custody if he buys me a brand-new red BMW convertible."

Although this may have been a more blatant approach than most, it's not unusual for moms to trade joint custody for financial concessions. In fact, in some states, the law used to be written in such a way that this type of wheeling-and-dealing was commonplace.

In the past, when a dad in Illinois wanted joint custody, the law made it clear that joint custody couldn't be awarded unless the mother agreed to it. Thus, moms could have control over this issue and could use it manipulatively if they so desired. The new law no longer requires a mother's consent, although some courts in Illinois, as well as other states, still honor the spirit of the old law. In fact, some attorneys for divorcing moms still suggest withholding consent to joint custody until they receive the support, money, and possessions they want.

I'm not advocating giving your wife everything you possess in order to gain joint custody, but do consider what you might provide her within reason in exchange for a good child-friendly joint custody agreement. Look for a way to provide her with additional support or something else that directly benefits the children. Your attorney can help you figure out what's appropriate to offer in these circumstances, as well as when to offer it. Good lawyers are skilled at knowing when the time is right to make an offer based on conversations with her lawyer.

Know the State's, County's, and Judge's Attitude Toward Joint Custody

Increasingly, states are recognizing the value of joint custody to children. If you happen to live in a state that leans in this direction, you have a better chance that the court will grant you this custody arrangement. As a general rule, the more liberal the state is, the more likely courts will favor joint custody, but there are a number of exceptions. Nevada, for instance, not known as a liberal state, has a predisposition toward joint custody.

More important, perhaps, are the rulings in the judicial circuit in which the divorce takes place. In Illinois, for instance, it's easier to win a joint custody ruling in Cook County rather than the southern part of the state.

The single most important factor to be aware of, though, is the attitude of a given judge. A veteran divorce attorney will be aware of a judge's rulings in the past regarding joint custody and the arguments that tend to sway a particular judge. It may be that one judge grants joint custody only when both parents are in complete agreement about a custody plan, and another judge may grant it even when moms resist (as long as the judge believes that the dad's relationship with a child is strong). Attorneys can also check a judge's political contributions, previous jobs, memberships, and so on to get a sense of where he or she stands on joint custody issues. In addition, savvy attorneys often know judges personally and are aware of issues that might influence their attitudes. I know one judge who was devastated when his wife kicked him out of the house and separated him from his children. As a result of this experience, he became much more empathetic toward divorcing dads who wanted joint custody. Although he always ruled on the merits of the case, he was completely unbiased with regard to gender, an attitude that benefited families and children.

If you believe you have a judge who is gender biased, your attorney can request a change. This is a highly situational matter, and you need to talk to your attorney about this tactic and weigh the pros and cons before taking action.

The Argument to Make to Moms or the Courts

It may be that even your offer of increased support payments or other financial or property concessions fails to sway your spouse to a joint custody arrangement. In some instances, moms are so furious at the dad that they will never give in on this issue. Some moms also suffer from psychological maladies, and it may be unrealistic to think that you can use reason and "best-interest-of-the-child" arguments on a woman who has a borderline personality disorder, among other challenges.

In the majority of cases, however, your wife may be willing to listen to reason if you present your argument for joint custody effectively. If she sincerely wants to do what is best for your children or realizes that she may jeopardize her own relationship with the kids, she may be willing to compromise on this point. If so, here are some strategies to consider:

- *Caution her about trying to use the "cooperation" ploy.* As I noted earlier, attorneys sometimes counsel moms to tell judges that they and their husbands can't cooperate on anything, even if it's not true, in order to convince them that joint custody isn't feasible. If this scenario is playing out in your divorce, talk to your attorney about taking countermeasures such as mediation, and then litigation, if needed. Many moms don't realize that this ploy can backfire; that if a judge determines that she's falsely stating that she and her spouse argue all the time, she could end up as the noncustodial parent. If you have evidence that she is trying to cut you out of your children's lives and you present that possibility to the court, she may be allowed only supervised visitation with the children. Obviously this evidence has to be strong and compelling, but many times, all it takes for moms to agree to joint custody is the realization of the repercussions for lying about the cooperation issue. In our electronic-dominated world, evidence often exists when a mom is trying to sabotage a child's relationship with her dad. Many text messages, e-mails, and other electronic communications are readily admissible in court, and if you have this type of evidence, it may provide enough negotiation leverage to help you obtain joint or even sole custody.

- *Communicate the financial and emotional benefits of joint custody.* Many divorcing women don't realize that joint custody can save them money. Invariably expenses arise relating to children over a period of years that aren't covered in the divorce agreement. Typically the custodial parent is responsible for these uncovered expenses: a twelve year old decides he wants to enroll in a martial arts school, or a fifteen year old starts studying French and requests a summer trip as part of a language-learning program, for example. When mom springs this new expense on the dad, he usually is upset, first and foremost because he wasn't part of the decision-making process. Consequently his anger causes him to say, "You never consulted me about this. I'm not paying."

In a well-written joint custody agreement, however, decisions are likely made together so dads feel as if they're part of the process. It's much more likely in these circumstances that they'll agree to split the costs evenly. In addition, a joint custody arrangement helps prevent at least some of the heated arguments that can occur over money. When the parents are continuously involved in making choices for their kids, they often find ways to compromise when they don't agree. Instead of dad feeling left out, resentful, and argumentative, he understands that he's still an equal partner in child raising and is calmer and more reasonable in his relationship with his ex.

• *Be creative about joint custody.* The courts are often remarkably flexible when it comes to joint custody arrangements. Contrary to what many people believe, joint custody doesn't have to mean the same thing for every set of parents. For instance, one of our clients was a truck driver who wanted joint custody. Unfortunately, his job required him to be on the road for much of the year, so it wasn't possible for him to be at every parent-teacher conference or to see his kids on a regular visitation schedule. We were able to craft an agreement in which shared decision making was focused on the health, education, and welfare of his kids. In addition, because the truck driver was on the road so much, we worked into the agreement an electronic visitation schedule designed to compensate for the time he couldn't be present physically with his kids, ages eleven and fourteen. Though he wasn't able to be physically present with his children as much as many other parents with joint custody agreements are, he had continuous access to them through cell phone, e-mail, and texting, as well as designated times for videoconferencing visits when he was on the road.

Being creative about joint custody may mean that you divvy up decision-making responsibilities according to your respective areas of expertise and interests. Maybe you're a former athlete who loves sports and your child's mom doesn't know or care about sports; the agreement can provide you with primary decision-making authority in this area. In exchange, you may cede your authority in another area where your ex has greater knowledge: as a musician, she's in charge of decisions regarding the instrument your daughter plays, as well as the private lessons she takes.

Similarly, the agreement doesn't have to adhere to a traditional visitation schedule. For instance, you can come up with an alternative schedule that gives you a more realistic chance of spending quality time with your children. Weekends may be bad for you; you may work one or both days, or maybe you have started another family and your new wife wants you to spend time with these children. There's nothing that prevents you from designating weekdays as times when you're with your children as long as their mom agrees with this schedule. Or if you're a teacher and you're extraordinarily busy during the school year, perhaps you can create an agreement that allows you to spend additional time with the children in the summer. You might take them camping for a week or two in the summer, for instance.

The point is that creativity will allow you to capitalize on the spirit of joint custody. It may also help you bolster your argument for joint custody, since the creative way you structure the agreement may suit not just you but the mom's schedule and requirements as well.

Sole Custody Agreements That Facilitate Involvement and Connection

It may be that you don't want or can't get joint custody for whatever reason. If this is the case, you can still craft a divorce agreement that will help you be a good divorced dad. Contrary to common belief, the key is not having a superaggressive lawyer who tries to bully a mom's lawyer in private negotiating sessions or in court. Instead, it's working with your lawyer to structure an agreement that is fair to you, to her, and especially to your children. If your attorney has significant experience creating these agreements for divorcing dads, he or she should be familiar with the following strategies. But you too should be aware of them so you can help your attorney work them into the agreement.

First, be as specific as possible in the agreement regarding your visitation or parenting schedule. Vagueness can hurt both moms and dads, but in many situations, vagueness tends to hurt dads more because courts still tend to lean to the mom's side when they interpret the language of agreements. In fact, it's not unusual for the mom's attorney to attempt to make the language vague on purpose, knowing that it will probably work in the mom's favor. This attorney may say something like, "Let's leave this part of the agreement kind of general for now, since we really don't know how things will be a year or two from now."

Never allow any vagueness in the agreement. Specify your parenting or visitation days and times. Detail the special occasion days (your birthday and Father's Day, for example) where you'd like to have your child with you. If you suspect that your wife will put the kids in day care for an excessive amount of time, you can place language in the agreement that limits that time to a certain number of hours. In addition, if you want the option of spending more time with your children, include a clause in the agreement that allows you the option to take the kids all or part of the time when they would otherwise be in day care. This gives you additional parenting time and saves your ex money.

Second, make sure you include a provision for an annual review. I know I've mentioned this earlier, but I want to reiterate it since it's so often overlooked (or some dads can't stand the thought of revisiting emotionally difficult issues annually). Situations change. At the time of the divorce, you may be working or your wife may be a stay-at-home mom. But in these volatile times, it's not unusual for this situation to reverse itself: she's working and you're not. In this instance, a review can give you the opportunity to gain more time with your kids when your wife is working. In addition, be sure to include a mandatory mediation clause for dispute resolution in addition to the review provision, again stipulating that no lawyers are to be present. If possible, name a mediator to be included in the agreement as well as an alternate mediator (if your first choice is unavailable, as sometimes happens). These provisions will facilitate adjusting to changing circumstances in ways that help you stay connected to your kids.

Third, include a radius clause in the agreement—one that defines a maximum relocation distance within the state where you and your ex reside that can't be exceeded without the written permission of the other parent or court order. Again, putting in a clause like this is often not even discussed, since at the time of the divorce, neither parent is thinking about moving away. But people can find themselves wanting to move because they are offered a great new job, are involved romantically with someone who lives elsewhere (or who decides to move), or are spiteful and this is way for the custodial parent to punish her ex. The simple omission of this clause can cause dads tremendous grief as they later find themselves too far away from their children to see them regularly. Many states allow one parent to relocate within the state, which is okay if you live in a geographically small state. If you live in, say, Texas or California, the distance between you and your kids can become prohibitively far.

Legal Reality Checks

Sometimes divorcing parents are so distraught or distracted during the divorce process that they lose sight of what's important. Dads may become so caught up in financial worries caused by the divorce or suffer from such low self-esteem that they don't think clearly about what they need to do for themselves and their children as the process unfolds. Therefore, consider the following three reality checks as ways to keep you focused on doing the right things for yourself and your children.

Reality Check #1: Are You Delaying Necessary Legal Action for Emotional Reasons?

You may tell yourself you need time before making decisions relating to your divorce. This is understandable on an emotional level, since it's tough to think straight about all the decisions you're facing when you're going through a difficult divorce. But what may be an appropriate emotional response isn't always an effective legal one. The reality is that delaying legal action can create a rift between you and your children in a number of ways.

You may accept whatever custody and visitation terms your wife dictates, even if you suspect they're unfair and will not allow you to see your child as much as you think is right. Or you may believe that the mom isn't abiding by the terms of the agreement but fail to challenge her on it in court. Or you may feel that she's neglecting your children but you do not take any legal action charging her with neglect. Or you may even be so depressed that you don't make an effort to establish a relationship with your child, accepting egregiously unfair stipulations that essentially cut off most contact with your son or daughter.

When you do finally decide you want to challenge your ex on the terms of the agreement or file a motion for neglect, the courts may well view you with a skeptical eye. They will wonder why it took you so long to take action, assuming that a concerned, committed parent would have responded to these issues right away and not let long periods of time pass before doing anything. The burden of proof, then, is on you. In addition, some dads lose touch when their exes and kids move away and the dads didn't challenge their relocation. In some instances, they may have difficulty even tracking their children down when they decide they want a relationship with them.

Divorce court judges place great value in maintaining the status quo. Earlier I referred to the importance of environmental stability in custody decisions. Judges believe that consistency and familiarity are important for the emotional health of children, and they hope their original order establishes a framework for a consistent, familiar life. When you challenge that order two or three years after it's issued, the judge is generally reluctant to change it. Their reasoning is that doing so could upset the status quo, creating chaos and confusion in a child's world, absent a substantial change in circumstances that it is in the best interest of the child to change custody.

Reality Check #2: Have You Read the Fine Print and Asked Questions Before You Sign on the Dotted Line?

Given your emotional state during the divorce, you may lack the patience or focus to want to read the divorce agreement yet another time or spend one extra minute in your lawyer's presence going over all the details. Yet I've seen father-child relationships suffer because dads didn't pay attention to everything in an agreement or failed to understand what a particular clause meant.

Here's a cautionary story to this point. Art was going through a tough divorce, battling tooth and nail with his wife about everything from division of marital property to support payments. After much negotiating, Art's lawyer had hammered out a marital settlement agreement that seemed fair. When it came time to sign the agreement, though, Art's wife's lawyer mentioned that some changes had been made. "Do I have to look at this thing again?" Art asked. His lawyer said no; just sign. Which Art did. Months later, Art received an order finding him in contempt for not abiding by the rules—rules that had been altered from the original version that Art had never read. This created a great deal of tension between Art and his ex and resulted in a number of legal problems that made Art even more depressed than he already was. For a number of months, Art barely saw his kids, and this resulted in an estrangement that has never been fully resolved.

Therefore, read everything as many times as necessary until you understand it and before you sign the divorce agreement. And ask, "What does this mean?" if there's anything you don't completely understand. Sometimes the legal language may be confusing, so don't be satisfied if you think you have a pretty good idea of what something means. Demand that your attorney translate it into lay terms and spell out what it means in terms of when you get to see your children, how long you get to spend with them, and so on. There is no such thing as a bad question.

Reality Check #3: Do You Have a Lawyer Who Understands and Is Willing to Protect Your Rights as a Father?

Don't be naive about attorneys. As in any other profession, there are good ones and bad ones. In your particular circumstance as a divorcing dad, a good attorney is someone who has extensive experience defending the rights of divorcing dads. When you meet with your attorney for the first time, pay attention to how or if he mentions your children. Does he seem concerned about doing what is best for them? Is he communicating clearly what you need to do to preserve your relationship with them? A lawyer who talks constantly about how aggressive he is and how he will make your wife pay for divorcing you may be pandering to your worst instincts.

In addition, never represent yourself. If you feel guilty, don't assuage your conscience by going without a lawyer. Remind yourself that your children may pay the cost of this act. Tell yourself that this is an adversarial process, and if your wife has an attorney and you don't, that attorney is likely to convince her to agree to terms that are not in your best interest. Unknowingly, you may agree to terms that provide you with less visitation than is your due, or worse.

Finally, the harsh reality is that the legal system still tilts toward moms and away from dads. If you are passive, naive, or distracted, you may be saddled with an agreement that places unwarranted restrictions on when and how often you see your kids or how involved you are in decisions that affect their lives. For this reason, I urge you to push distracting emotions aside and pay attention to every aspect of the divorce process. It might be difficult to do now, but you'll be grateful you did for years to come.

CHAPTER 9

Going Forward

*How to Maintain and Strengthen
Connections with Your Kids*

You may implement all the suggestions in this book, and they may help you establish a terrific relationship with your kids. Things may go well for weeks or months or years, and then something happens. Maybe you lose your job, fall behind on support payments, or become ill, and you stop seeing your kids because you can't face them. Maybe your ex remarries and dashes your faint hopes that you might get back together with her. Maybe she starts making your visits with your kids a nightmare: she deliberately tells you the wrong time or place to pick them up, denies you the chance to see them on your regular day because she's punishing you for some reason, or gets them all riled up before your visit so there's a lot of tension when you see them.

These or other challenges await at least some of you, and to continue to be a good father, you need to meet them with strength and information. In this chapter, I hope to give you the latter so that you can muster the former.

Although many different events and situations can arise that challenge your ability to be a good dad, the following are the ones you're most likely to face.

Mom Starts Playing Visitation Games

It's not unusual for moms to abide by the visitation terms for a period of time, but something happens that causes them to use visitation as a tool of revenge against you. It may be as simple as your remarrying and your ex feeling the hurt of the initial break-up all over again. She feels hurt and wants to hurt you in return. Or perhaps she still abides by the letter of the visitation terms but violates the spirit. In other words, she sabotages visits with your kids. For instance, she lies to them about something you said or did, causing them to be angry with you and making the visit tense; or she calls them on the phone repeatedly during your visit, interrupting your time with them.

Some dads become so frustrated with their ex-spouse's visitation machinations that they miss some visitation days or are so furious with her that they're not emotionally present when they are with their kids. One way or another, they allow this game playing to disturb their relationship with their children—which is exactly what these moms want.

If you are in this situation, talk to your lawyer about what's going on. If your ex is violating the visitation clause in your agreement, gather evidence of these violations, and your attorney can use this information to regain your rights. If her violations are less direct, you should still tell your attorney about them, and he or she can advise you whether it's worth pursuing legally. Many times, it's possible to gather evidence of these indirect but no less destructive actions and use them to regain your visitation rights.

Under no circumstance should you let either direct or indirect game playing interfere with your relationship with your children. In fact, don't let your ex see you angry about it or missing visitation because of it. Force yourself to appear unaffected by what she's doing. If she sees she's not hurting you or your relationship with your children, she may stop these behaviors on her own.

Mom Relocates

Your ex might move across town or to another city hundreds of miles away or at the opposite side of the state. (As I noted in the previous chapter, the custodial parent may be able to move anywhere within the state if your divorce agreement does not have a radius clause.) Even if she just moves ten or twenty miles away, it may be distant enough to discourage you from visiting your children as much as you would like. You may be snowed under at work trying to keep your job and find it difficult to travel a greater distance. Psychologically, too, the increased distance may feel burdensome—it's just one too many irritating events.

If your ex moves farther away with the children, you have a number of options to maintain your connection with them, including these:

- Use more electronic communication (e-mail, text, and videoconferencing, for example) if it's logistically difficult to keep traveling to the new residence.
- Suggest compensating for the increased travel difficulty by having the kids stay more often at your place—in the summer, for long weekends, and whenever else is convenient based on their schedule and that of their mom.
- Move closer to their new location if possible. I realize that it's not always possible for a number of reasons, but you may have nothing keeping you in your current residence.

Your Kids (Especially Adolescents) Rebel Against You

You feel that your kids hate you. They call you names, accuse you of abandoning them, suggest that you destroyed the family, and say and do one hundred things that make you feel guilty about the divorce. This most often happens when your children are adolescents. Adolescence is a difficult age, not just for kids but for most parents, and divorce often increases the difficulty. But you need to remind yourself that this too shall pass. Communicate the hurt you feel to your kids when they act badly toward you, but don't get into the sort of hostile battles that further alienate both of you. Express what you're feeling without hostility, and then let it go.

A number of divorced dads who feel guilty about the divorce and are attacked by their kids for destroying the family say that it helps when they remind themselves that the family was being destroyed not by them but by the marriage—by the constant battles between themselves and the kids' mom. Staying married would not have done the children any favors, and the divorce should give each parent time to regain a degree of emotional health—health that can help them be better parents.

At the same time, you need to be alert for signs of parental alienation. If your ex is mounting a campaign of denigration to make your children hate you, then you have every right to take legal action against her. Listening to what your children say will give you a sense of whether their mom is feeding them false information about you and the marriage. Listen to what friends and family tell you too: they may know that your ex is trying to disconnect you from the kids. Your lawyer can advise you on what evidence you need to gather to go back to court and take action against an alienator.

You Lose Your Job and Struggle to Make Support Payments

Losing a job and being unable to support your children financially is devastating to many men because they've been raised to believe that this is an almost sacred responsibility. In some instances, dads want to punish themselves (unconsciously) for falling behind in their support payments. As a result, they can't bear to face their children and decide to stay away until they get a new job and are able to resume payments.

This is the worst thing you can do if this happens to you. As difficult as this situation is, all you can do is try to find work and be frugal. Until your financial situation improves, look at joblessness as an opportunity to see your children more. Ask your ex if she's willing to let you take care of the children instead of paying a sitter or child care center. Don't forget that you may be able to petition the court successfully for an abated or lowered support payment while you are unemployed.

Mom Brings a Stepfather or Other Male Parental Figure into Your Children's Lives

It's one thing if another man is the cause of the divorce and you have to deal with this issue from the beginning. The anger can wash over you like a tidal wave and swamp your life. The divorce process, though, can be cathartic and allow you to vent your feelings—to your lawyer and a therapist, ideally—and in time you recover.

A more insidious problem can be when you go along for a year or two and neither you nor your ex develops a relationship with another person. You get into a rhythm of relating to each other as divorced parents, and things proceed smoothly. Then another man enters the picture and upsets the rhythm you've established. It's not as much that you're jealous of your ex, but you are pained by the attention he receives from your children. It seems as if they feel he's way cooler than you are. Perhaps he has a fancier car or a more interesting job. Whatever the reason, you feel as if he's usurping your place in the family.

Before jumping to false conclusions and allowing them to disconnect you from your kids, recognize a truth I elaborated on in Chapter Six: blood is thicker than water. Biological dads are connected to their kids at a very deep level. The thousands of dads I've represented have had many factors that have separated them from their children: jail, relocation on the other side of the world, parental alienation, and more. But in the vast majority of the cases, these dads were able to maintain strong, ongoing relationships with their children unless they (the dads) became absent.

Recognize, too, the term psychologists use: *habituation*. The cool new boyfriend won't seem so cool to your children as they become habituated to him. Over time he will probably never be anything more than a second parental figure. If you hang in there and work at keeping close to your kids, you'll increase the odds of your being the primary father figure.

CHAPTER 10

Developing Trends and Changes That Still Need to Be Made

In certain ways, being a good divorced dad is easier now than ever before. E-mail, cell phones, and texting facilitate communication with children even when it's difficult to see them (and some kids prefer electronic communication for conversing). Similarly, social norms now make it acceptable for dads to stay at home with their children, express their feelings, and be more involved with every aspect of a child's life. And legal norms acknowledge the importance of dads as parent; no longer are moms automatically given custody. The courts are much more cognizant of the importance of father involvement in kids' lives, and whether through joint custody or visitation, they try to foster this involvement as being in the best interest of children.

Developing Trends

At the same time, trends are developing that bear watching, since they can affect your ability to be a good divorced dad. Here are some key ones you should be aware of.

A More Subtle Form of Gender Bias

Overt gender bias still exists. In fact, relatively recently I had a case in which my client was getting divorced from a woman who was a drug abuser and had seriously injured one of their kids. The judge, however, was reluctant to give my client custody even though my client was an upstanding citizen.

Now, however, gender bias often emerges in more subtle forms. Judges want to present themselves as gender neutral, and so they are much less likely than in the past to award custody to a mom who doesn't deserve it over a dad who does. However, some judges find other ways to act on their biases. For instance, in one case, I was representing a dad in a custody case, and it was clear to everyone in the courtroom that the dad deserved custody. The judge called me into chambers and told me that I was winning the case but cautioned me that if I continued to insist that the mother should not have custody, he would take the kids away from both parents rather than award sole custody to the dad. The judge felt that it was wrong for dads to have custody under any circumstances. At the same time, he was not going to make a ruling that communicated his bias; he preferred encouraging me to settle for joint custody.

Subtle gender bias can also emerge in mediation. Mediators may push both parents toward compromises that favor mom over dad in certain particulars. For instance, a mediator may discourage dad's desire to care for his small children while their mom is working instead of incurring the expense of day care. The mediator may believe (consciously or not) that it's not a man's place to do this; instead he should be working or at least looking for a job.

The mediator may also subscribe to the old gender-biased stereotype that "men are biological necessities but social accidents."

Be aware, then, that you may confront bias at any point during or after the divorce, but that it may not appear to be obvious bias. Many times, the bias is like the "tie goes to the runner" baseball rule. In this instance, though, the runner is the mom. If all things are equal, a judge is still likely to rule in favor of the mom over the dad. If the dad can present only a fair case for joint custody, for example, the odds are probably that he will not get it if the judge is biased.

More Female Judges

This may seem like a negative trend from a gender bias standpoint, but it's actually the opposite. A number of male judges bend over backward to be fair to moms; they want to demonstrate that they aren't biased in favor of men. But some of them bend too far and inadvertently are guilty of gender bias.

The increasing number of female judges, however, is leading to less gender bias. Many of these judges are also moms, and they are keenly aware of the needs of children. As a result, many look at what's best for the children, and that supersedes all other considerations. In many areas, female judges now outnumber males.

Continuing Debate over Parental Alienation

As more and more courts recognize the existence of parental alienation, that is, one parent turning a child against the other parent, divorced dads and their children have benefited. When either parent engages in this behavior—and both moms and dads do—it has a negative impact on kids. Parental alienation is not gender specific. But it's most often a weapon wielded by the custodial parent, and moms are more often custodial parents than dads are.

For many years, the courts didn't acknowledge the existence of this syndrome; it was assumed that both parents might occasionally say negative things about each other but that this was the nature of divorce and its aftermath. In recent years, however, mounting evidence of parental alienation has been discovered, and the courts have increasingly ruled against parents in custody hearings when they've tried to alienate the children against the other parent.

Nonetheless, we're seeing a growing debate about this issue. A PBS documentary, *Breaking the Silence*, suggested that abusive dads use false charges of parental alienation to wrest custody from moms and that this syndrome doesn't exist.[1] I've appeared before judges who have been dismissive of the concept of parental alienation.

But there is so much evidence of its existence that questioning it seems absurd. Forensic psychiatrist Richard A. Gardner identified parental alienation syndrome in the 1980s and is one of the leading experts on it. In addition, a study conducted by Stanley S. Clawar and Brynne Valerie Rivlin followed seven hundred high-conflict divorce cases over a twelve-year period. Clawar and Rivlin found that elements of parental alienation were present in the vast majority of the cases they studied.[2]

But one of the best and most compelling descriptions of parental alienation is provided by Wayne Halick, a private detective who works with our law firm. An attorney asked him to observe our client, a divorced dad, with his ex-wife and children in a fast food restaurant. Wayne was seated nearby and watched as the mom and kids entered the restaurant for the custody exchange. Here is an excerpt from what Wayne observed:

> When the mother and the children entered the McDonald's, she appeared to be using her hands and body to shield the boys as if they were approaching a dangerous situation while the children were trying to see their father. They were obviously much shorter than their mother but couldn't seem to get past her. The father was waving from across the restaurant. The older son saw him, smiled, and began to wave back. As soon as he started to wave, the mother grabbed him by the back of his coat,

pulled him toward her, and got down on one knee. She shook her finger in his face as if she were scolding him. He lowered his chin to his chest and flushed. Both boys then proceeded to meekly approach their father, being careful to stay behind their mother. When the mother was approximately twenty feet from the father, she began to yell at him. Several patrons in the area appeared to be uncomfortable, and one of the cashiers stopped taking an order to see what the commotion was all about. The entire restaurant seemed to stop for a moment. The mother told the father that she had to force the children to come with her because they were afraid to see him. The boys continued to keep their heads down and continued to do so until the mother exited the restaurant. The mother made several comments about the father not loving the children, being a deadbeat, and not caring about them.

Wayne added that the father remained calm during this exchange and the kids seemed to come to life once their mother departed. They were apparently afraid of their mom, not their dad.

Don't let anyone tell you that parental alienation is a fiction, and if you're a victim, consult with your attorney about it. If the charge is proved, it can change the outcome of a custody hearing. Certainly you should consult with your attorney and share what you've observed, and he or she can help you determine if provable alienation exists. Here are some common behaviors associated with the syndrome:

- Name-calling in front of the children
- Accusations that one parent doesn't love the kids
- Blaming for breaking up the family
- Denigrating tone of voice
- Dismissive gestures
- Words or gestures that indicate to the kids that they should be afraid of the parent

- Lying to prevent the dad from seeing the children during court-approved visitation periods
- Failing to let the dad know about key events in the child's life so he doesn't attend them

Changes That Need to Be Made

Over the years, I've given many talks about divorce and dads, and some of them have been at Stateville Correctional Center and Cook County Jail in Illinois. I've talked to inmates who are fathers, and a number of these men tell me that they left their children before being incarcerated and aren't going to reconnect with them when they are released because they love them. They believe that their absence will help rather than hurt their sons and daughters. I'm not excusing the behavior of these men, but the fact is that at least some of them have been brainwashed by society. They've been told that they're no good, that they're worthless, that kids need their moms but not their dads. In numerous different ways, they've learned that they are biological necessities but social accidents.

Certainly inmates have reasons to feel badly about themselves, but they don't see that despite the mistakes they've made, they can have value as fathers. They don't realize how much their children may need them no matter what they've done in the past. Society has sent them a message that they've taken to heart, and that's sad.

What's even sadder is that this message is sent to all men, not just dads who have made mistakes in their lives. They are dads who have never committed any crimes, in fact are upstanding citizens, yet after a divorce, they too feel that their children will be better off without them. Or at the very least, they believe that the mom is far more important to the children than they are.

This is the attitude that must change so that dads can be physically and emotionally present in their children's lives. We need everyone from teachers to politicians to religious leaders communicating that dads and moms are equally important as parents. We need to start a national dialogue on this subject, and I hope this book lends itself to that goal.

Beyond that, three tangible changes can help divorcing dads be more involved as parents.

Expand Mediation

We need to expand the use of mediation in divorce cases involving minor children. Although mediation certainly is used in jurisdictions throughout the country, it is not used as frequently and broadly as it should be. Even in some cases where mediation is supposed to be automatic when contested custody issues are involved, it still must be requested, and attorneys sometimes fail to request it in a timely manner or at all.

Mediation also tends to be limited to custody, excluding important related issues. It could be more effective if used to deal with everything from dependency exemptions to support conflicts that often can't be ignored in mediating custody disputes because they are integral to these disputes. If mediation were more broadly applied, it would be more effective, and we could not only avoid a lot of costly litigation but also avoid some of the animosity between parents that litigation often produces (not to mention the draining of funds that could be better used to support the kids). In addition, in some areas of the country, mediation isn't paid for by the government. As a result, many parents decline mediation because they consider it an additional, unaffordable expense. In some instances, dads just do what moms want, refusing not only to hire a mediator but an attorney to represent them as well, and they often end up with their parenting rights diminished.

Finally, we need a system that ensures experienced, gender-neutral mediators. Mediation's effectiveness is predicated on having a competent mediator. This means that they should not only have the proper training and skills but also the right mind-set to be a mediator.

Encourage Premarital Counseling

Couples should talk to a coach or therapist about what marriage and parenting require and the hot-button issues that might already exist prior to marriage. Premarital counseling could serve the same purpose as preventative medicine: helping people realize that marriage might be a mistake or alerting them about the realities of marriage and helping them address potential conflicts in advance. I realize that during the honeymoon period of relationships, people often can't imagine the problems that can arise because of kids and divorce, but this is an important discussion. At the very least, parents should agree verbally that they will be equally responsible for raising their children no matter what happens down the line. Psychologically, this commitment might help dads as well as moms feel bound to be active participants in their children's lives.

Make Joint Custody the Norm

Third, and perhaps most important, every state law should have the presumption that joint custody is in the best interests of the children. If this presumption existed, the courts would give far more parents equal rights and responsibilities for raising their children, creating an incentive to negotiate rather than litigate. This doesn't mean that as many dads as moms should have physical custody of kids—for many reasons, more kids will stay in their mom's residence than in their dad's—but they should share in decisions concerning their children and be given regular opportunities to be with and communicate with his kids.

As a veteran divorce attorney, I'm not naive about any of these issues. I know that change happens slowly when it comes to legislative reform and especially to laws governing divorce. But I'm also optimistic that we're seeing a slow but discernible shift in the country's consciousness about the importance of fathers. In minority and urban communities, seminars and conferences are being held promoting father involvement. Everyone from

President Obama to Reverend Jesse Jackson to Congressman Danny K. Davis from Illinois has spoken out on this issue.

I think we're also beginning to recognize that father absence isn't just a problem for the cities or minorities. Obviously it's a significant problem for these groups, but many affluent, white, suburban men are facing some form of parenting challenge, be it physical or emotional absence—or it may simply be that that their involvement is erratic.

I've represented thousands of divorcing dads over the years, and the vast majority of them want to be present in their kids' lives. More than anything else, they want to attend all of their kids' sports activities and teacher conferences; they want to have them stay over at their place and want to talk to them on a regular basis about their problems and successes. Too often, though, they're discouraged by societal messages, gender bias, and an unresponsive legal system. Like the incarcerated fathers, they rationalize why their kids don't need them around all the time or why they're better off without them.

This has to change, and I'm confident it will. Being a father is a sacred responsibility, and most men take on this role with great seriousness. And we should never forget that any man's loss of a child diminishes all of humanity. While the turmoil of divorce may confuse some men about this role temporarily, most fathers just need a bit of guidance and support to get back on track and be good divorced dads. I trust this book will provide at least some of that guidance.

Abuse Excuse, http://www.abuse-excuse.com
For adults unjustly accused of child abuse. "ABUSE-EXCUSE.COM
provides resource information, child abuse books, and more to parents
and others wrongly accused, falsely accused of child abuse, physical child
abuse (including Shaken Baby Syndrome), child neglect, sexual
child abuse, child pornography via the Internet, 'repressed' memories,
sexual harassment, or domestic violence (spousal abuse). We aim to
help the falsely and wrongly accused to articulate scientific facts to child
protection investigators, teachers, attorneys and judges, urging them to
exercise caution in their 'rush to judge' abuse calls. About 2/3 of all child
abuse reports turn out to be unfounded, as errors or mistakes in professional judgment."

Academic Development Institute, http://www.adi.org
"The Academic Development Institute (ADI) works with families,
schools, and communities so that all children may become self-directed
learners, avid readers, and responsible citizens, respecting themselves
and those around them. ADI's vision is of an American landscape filled
with distinct school communities reflecting the hopes and dreams of the
people intimately attached to them. To this image of the school as a
community, ADI is devoted."

Administration for Children and Families, http://www.acf.hhs.gov
"The Administration for Children and Families, part of the United
States Department of Health and Human Services, brings together
in one organization, the broad range of Federal programs that address
the needs of children and families. These programs are at the heart of the
Federal effort to strengthen families and to assist all children to succeed
by bringing new ideas, insights, and leadership directly to bear on the
issues that impact the lives of all Americans."

Fatherhood Educational Institute, http://fatherhood-edu.org
The institute promotes positive fatherhood involvement in poverty-stricken communities. It is here to help fathers. It does not hold lavish dinners and expensive fundraisers to pay for their staff, marketing, or expenses.

Fathers & Families Coalition of America, Inc., http://www.fathers andfamiliescoalition.org
"FFCA has a mission to enhance the capacity of service providers throughout the nation, so they will be better equipped to effectively serve fathers, mothers, and children."

Fatherville Forum, http://www.fatherville.com
"We are a resource for fathers . . . by fathers and about fathers. We are here to encourage and support dads as they make their journey down the road called fatherhood."

Illinois Council on Responsible Fatherhood, http://responsiblefather hood.illinois.gov
The Illinois state legislature created this commission to promote the positive involvement of both parents in the lives of their children. Its mission is to help more children in Illinois grow up with a responsible father in their lives.

National Adoption Center, http://www.adopt.org
"The National Adoption Center expands adoption opportunities for children living in foster care throughout the United States, and is a resource to families and to agencies who seek the permanency of caring homes for children."

National Association of State Boards, http://nasbe.org
"The National Association of State Boards of Education exists to strengthen State Boards as the preeminent educational policymaking bodies for students and citizens. NASBE is the only National Organization giving voice and adding value to the nation's State Boards of Education."

National Parent Teacher Association, http://www.pta.org
"As the largest volunteer child advocacy association in the nation, Parent Teacher Association (PTA) reminds our country of its obligations to children and provides parents and families with a powerful

voice to speak on behalf of every child while providing the best tools for parents to help their children be successful students."

U.S. Department of Health and Human Services, www.hhs.gov
This U.S. government agency safeguards the health of all Americans and offers key human services, especially for those who are in need of assistance.

NOTES

Introduction
1. J. Fields, *The Living Arrangements of Children* (Washington, D.C.: U.S. Census Bureau, 2001).

Chapter Two
1. D. Blankenhorn, *Fatherless America* (New York: Basic Books, 1995).

Chapter Three
1. P. R. Amato, "Life-Span Adjustment of Children to Their Parents' Divorce," *Future of Children*, 1994, 4(1), 413–416.
2. S. H. Howell, P. R. Portes, and J. H. Brown, "Gender and Age Differences in Child Adjustment to Parent Separation," *Journal of Divorce and Remarriage*, 1997, 27, 141–158.
3. L. Neher and J. Short, "Risk and Protective Factors for Children's Substance Use and Antisocial Behavior Following Parental Divorce," *American Journal of Orthopsychiatry*, 1998, 68, 154–161.

Chapter Five
1. The quotation is from a motivational poster, "Priorities Boy," produced by Successories of Illinois.
2. U.S. Government Accounting Office, "Interstate Child Support," report GAO/HRD-92-39FS (Washington, D.C.: U.S. Government Accounting Office, January 1992).

Chapter Six
1. M. Daly and M. Wilson, "A Reply to Gelles: Stepchildren Are Disproportionately Abused, and Diverse Forms of Violence Can Share Causal Factors," *Human Nature*, 1991, 2(4), 419–426.
2. M. Fine and L. Kurdek, "Parenting Cognitions in Stepfamilies: Differences Between Parents and Stepparents and Relations to Parenting Satisfaction," *Journal of Social and Personal Relationships*, 1994, 11, 95–112.

3. E. Cooksey and M. Fondell, "Spending Time with His Kids: Effects of Family Structure on Fathers' and Children's Lives," *Journal of Marriage and the Family*, 1996, 58, 693–707.

Chapter Ten
1. D. Lasseur (producer), *Breaking the Silence*. PBS, 2005.
2. S. S. Clawar and B. V. Rivlin, *Children Held Hostage: Dealing with Programmed and Brainwashed Children* (Chicago: American Bar Association, 1991).

INDEX